Philip M. Pedley

THE ATATÜRK INTERVIEW

Armenian Tall Tales or an Inconvenient Truth?

ЧҺ

Gomidas Institute
London

ISBN 978-1-909382-43-5

Gomidas Institute
42 Blythe Rd.
London W14 0HA
United Kingdom
www.gomidas.org
info@gomidas.org

If a man will stand up and assert, and repeat and reassert, that two and two do not make four, I know nothing in the power of argument that can stop him.
– ABRAHAM LINCOLN, speech at Peoria, Illinois, in reply to Senator Douglas, October 16, 1854

CONTENTS

Introduction

This paper establishes the provenance of a purported interview with Turkish President Mustafa Kemal [Atatürk] by Karl Emil Hildebrand published in the *Los Angeles Examiner* in 1926. The significance of the interview is twofold. Firstly, Mustafa Kemal's acknowledgement of Turkish culpability in Armenian massacres and secondly his revelation that a hitherto unknown high-level female informant thwarted the 1926 Izmir assassination attempt on his life.

Although the interview has been cited by leading scholars writing on the issue as evidence of a genocide, the credibility of the source has been undermined by research conducted by Professor Turkkaya Ataöv. Ataöv asserts that neither the journalist, nor the press agency that syndicated the interview existed. Moreover, he maintains that the tone of Ataturk's comments and other factual elements are not authentic and the cumulative effect is to prove beyond doubt that the article is a crude falsification by the Armenian community to appropriate the good name of Mustafa Kemal Atatürk.

New evidence, revealed here, establishes the provenance of the interview. Mustafa Kemal's acknowledgement of Ottoman guilt is confirmed. This research refutes the charge of falsification by establishing that there was a contemporary Swedish journalist called Hildebrand with an interest in eastern affairs. Even more significantly, Hildebrand's son-in-law was the Chairman of the League of Nations committee set up to arbitrate on Turkish and British claims on Mosul in the 1920s.

In examining the account of attempted assassination, this paper contends that the woman conspirator who alerted Mustafa Kemal to the Izmir assassination plot was his wartime compatriot and Turkey's leading feminist, Edib Halide. She was at the centre of the political machinations of the opposition People's Republican Party and aware of the impending assassination. Her late change of heart and confession explains why Mustafa Kemal abruptly halted the presidential train mid-route to Izmir. As such it challenges the prevailing narrative that Mustafa Kemal exploited the attempted assassination to silence innocent PRP members.

The Background

In 2008 Turkish academic Turkayya Ataöv published the results of his research into "striking falsifications" surrounding "the Armenian Issue".[1] In his view fabricated evidence had been cited as proof of Turkish recognition of Ottoman culpability in delivering genocide. These alleged fabrications were distributed to the US Congress and public opinion formers.[2] Any claims of fabrication should be taken seriously, especially as Ataöv himself occupies the role of something akin to an official Turkish State historian. As such he has been deployed as an expert witness to counter charges of Ottoman genocide.[3] In that capacity he has attended a number of international forums to state the anti-genocide viewpoint. A Turkish Government biography claims he has presented evidence to "two Paris courts, four European Parliament meetings and thirty-three United Nations sessions as a specialist of the field."[4]

Ataöv was particularly keen to disprove that the founding father of the Turkish Republic and first president, Mustafa Kemal Atatürk himself, had acknowledged the genocidal crimes of the Young Turk regime. At issue is a disputed syndicated interview with Mustafa

1 Türkkaya. Ataöv, *Armenian Falsifications* (New York: Okey Enterprises Inc, 2008), p. 56.
2 Ibid.
3 Fatma Muge Gocek, *Denial of Violence: Ottoman Past, Turkish Present, and Collective Violence against the Armenians, 1789-2009* (Oxford University Press, 2014), p. 604, note 146.
4 Turkey Ministry of Culture, "Ataöv, Türkkaya," http://www.kultur.gov.tr/EN,118279/ataov-turkkaya.html. Accessed 2/2/2016.

Kemal carried in a US newspaper report, known as the 'Hildebrand Interview'. In Ataöv's words, "some Armenian circles have been resorting to this article, expecting others to believe *a priori* that the words have fallen from the mouth of the Turkish leader. They provide no evidence at all..."[1]

The interview was allegedly conducted by a foreign correspondent with Mustafa Kemal in the immediate aftermath of the 1926 Izmir attempt on the President's life. Ataöv contends that a number of elements prove the Hildebrand interview was fabricated by Armenians. In support of his claim, Ataöv examines the character of Mustafa Kemal and concludes the intemperate language in the interview is not in keeping with his persona. Nor are the hostile views attributed to Mustafa Kemal in respect of his rival Enver Paşa. In addition, Ataöv asserts there are no official records of such an interview, nor any similar reports in the Turkish domestic press. Moreover, Ataöv contends the events describing the assassination are incorrect, since the interview mentions a female informer rather than the standard narrative that identifies a male conspirator. Perhaps more damaging still, Ataöv asserts that following his extensive research, the press agency from which the story emanated did not exist and neither did the journalist.

The fabrication assertions have been repeated ad nauseam by Ataöv in other journals and in various lecture tours of the US and UK.[2] In turn, other genocide skeptics including academics and partisan Turkish interest groups have cited Ataöv's claims about the interview as definitive proof of an Armenian fabrication.[3] For scholars in the opposite camp, the effect of Ataöv's piece was to throw doubt on the

1 Ataöv, p. 55.
2 Türkkaya Ataöv, *The "Armenian Question": Conflict, Trauma & Objectivity* (Center for Strategic Research, 1999), pp. 150-51.
3 Gürbüz Sevgi Zübeyde, "Some More Ugly Lies About Ataturk," *Turkish Journal* Online Edition 11/08/07 (2007). Accessed 2/2/2016. Holdwater, "Ataturk's 1926 "Interview" Proven as Forgery," http://www.tall armeniantale.com/forger-Emile1926.htm.

Hildebrand interview. Despite this, some scholars on the Armenian issue continue to cite the Hildebrand Interview.[1] Indeed, leading Armenian studies expert Vahakn Dadrian includes the Hildebrand Interview as one of his key Turkish sources.[2] However, other academics have been obliged to acknowledge the effect of Ataöv's research by either removing it as a reliable source or as in the case of Taner Akçam, qualifying his citation by an acknowledgement of its contested status amongst Turkish scholars.[3] Noted expert on Turkish history, Eric Zürcher also cites the Hildebrand interview but acknowledges the doubts "about the authenticity and reliability of the text…" raised by Ataöv's research.[4]

The Hildebrand interview is potentially a key point of evidence. There is limited documentary evidence relating to the attitude of Mustafa Kemal to the Armenian massacres and each are subjected to fierce scrutiny by Turkish scholars keen to disprove any acknowledgement of culpability by such a venerated figure.

Taner Akçam relied on Mustafa Kemal's reference to a "shameful act," (providing the title of Akçam's seminal work on the Armenian Genocide) to make the case for his acknowledgement. However, the context of these words is now disputed and with it the inference that Mustafa Kemal acknowledged the massacres and was critical of those who committed them.[5] The relevance of the 1926 Hildebrand

---

1 Cathie Carmichael, "Was Religion Important in the Destruction of Ancient Communities in the Balkans, Anatolia and Black Sea Regions, C. 1870–1923?," *Southeast European and Black Sea Studies* 7, no. 3 (2007): p. 366.
2 Vahakn N Dadrian, *Documentation of the Armenian Genocide in Turkish Sources* (Institute on the Holocaust and Genocide, 1991), p. 131.
3 Taner Akçam, *A Shameful Act: The Armenian Genocide and the Question of Turkish Responsibility* (Macmillan, 2006), p. 249.
4 Erik Jan Zürcher, "A Question of Genocide: Armenians and Turks at the End of the Ottoman Empire," ed. Ronald Grigor Suny, Fatma Müge Göçek, and Norman M Naimark (Oxford: Oxford University Press, 2011), p. 314.
5 Fatma Ulgen, "Reading Mustafa Kemal Atatürk on the Armenian Genocide of 1915," *Patterns of Prejudice* 44, no. 4 (2010): pp. 380-83.

interview therefore is whether it buttresses the view that Mustafa Kemal disapproved of, and thereby acknowledged the Armenian massacres. This paper examines the fabrication allegations and establishes the factual basis for believing the authenticity of the Hildebrand interview.

The Interview & the Nercessian Covering Note

The person who discovered the Hildebrand interview in the *Los Angeles Examiner* archives was an Armenian émigré by the name of Nishan Nercessian, a resident of Los Angeles. In introducing the article to the wider world, Nercessian typed a covering note that Ataöv suggests is proof of fabrication since the opening sentence allegedly contains a nonsensical chronological error.[1] Nercessian wrote:

> This reproduction [the interview] from the *Los Angeles Examiner* of August 1, 1926, is an article written by the founder in 1923 and President of the Turkish Republic, Mustafa Kemal Pasha who later took the title Ataturk.[2]

Ataöv states this statement is "doubly absurd" since Nercessian is claiming the article was written in 1923, but the assassination to which the article refers did not occur until 1926. In fact Nercessian is not claiming the words attributed to Mustafa Kemal were written in 1923 as quick re-reading of the text confirms. It is clear that Nercessian is attributing the interview and words to Mustafa Kemal, "...*the founder in 1923 and President of the Turkish Republic*..." Since the Turkish Republic was indeed founded in 1923 and Mustafa Kemal was indeed its first President, the sentence is factual.[3] It is difficult to understand why such an obtuse interpretation was placed on them.

---

1 Ataöv, p. 56.
2 Nercessian, Nishan Covering note to the Hildebrand Interview. Published by the Zoryan Institute.
3 See official Turkish Gov website for founding of Turkish Republic. http://www.mfa.gov.tr/turkiye-cumhuriyeti-disisleri-bakanligi-tarihcesi.en.mfa. Accessed 10/2/2018.

Leaving aside the matter of Ataöv's misunderstanding of Nercessian's note and grammatical construction, more serious challenges are made by him concerning the validity of the Hildebrand interview itself. These challenges relate to the content of the Hildebrand Interview and the circumstances/status of those individuals and entities said to have been involved in its production. Those issues highlighted include the news agency, the newspaper, and the journalist. All of these are held to be suspicious in some way by Ataöv.

A full transcript of the Hildebrand interview is reproduced below:

KEMAL PROMISES MORE HANGINGS OF POLITICAL ANTAGONISTS IN TURKEY

President Says He Will Forgive Woman, Once His Friend, Who Joined Conspirators
By Mustapha Kemal Pasha

(The Dictator of Turkey, in an interview with Emile Hildebrand, a Swiss artist and journalist, on June 22)

I shall not stop until every guilty person, no matter how high his rank, has been hung from the gallows as a grim warning to all incipient plotters against the security of the Turkish Republic. Since the very hour of its reincarnation in the rejuvenated body of the Republic, our nation has endured travails no other nation has ever experienced.

When we were fighting external enemies, or enemies whom we were certain were sympathetic with foreign intriguers, nearly all of the rank and file of our population were enthusiastically, even fanatically, united to deliver the nation from the multiple foreign yokes. But no sooner had the nation proved its worth to its foreign detractors than certain elements, bred in the old school of political intrigue, began to show their claws. We were face to face with a menace to the life of the republic from two elements.

One was the group who combined religious fanaticism and ignorance with political imbecility and who, in the past, under different Sultans had come to believe that the state was an organism to be exploited through debauchery, corruption and brazen bribery for personal ends. I put the ax in the dual root of this sinister and reprehensible theory of government by destroying the Khalif and the Sultan. I sent into exile the persons in whom this theory was personified. Large numbers, adherents of this school of politics, attempted to interpret any act as atheistic, and, under the aegis of religion, began to intrigue against the life of the republic.

SIXTY LEADERS HANG AT DAWN

In several instances in the past when, in Kurdistan and other interior regions of Anatolia, they showed a disposition to challenge the will of the republic, I crushed them with an iron hand, and, for example, had over sixty of their leaders hanged at dawn.

That element had its lesson and will not again attempt to measure swords with me.

The second element, I am now about to deal with ruthlessly, is the group of men who in the pre-republic days were known in the world as the Committee of the Union of the Young Turks. The ranks of this element were recruited from a questionable assortment of political adventurers, half-educated progressives and men of dissolute habits. In the days when we were battling against foes from within and without, this element joined us and fought in our ranks. Yet from the early days I had misgivings as to their motives. But I wished, hoped and then prayed that once our country was redeemed from the foreign yoke, this element would mend its methods and become infused with the zeal of patriotism. I soon began to realise that my hopes were doomed to be disillusioned and my prayers were to be unanswered. I patiently waited, keeping a sharp eye on their movements.

SEDITIOUS MOVEMENTS CLOAKED

They formed themselves into a political opposition. I do not pretend to be a dictator, bent to suppress sincere and honest political opposition, because a republic is a misnomer when it ceases to brook criticism. But when a group of dissolute, corrupt and unscrupulous political adventurers begin to organise seditious movements under the cloak of political opposition, it becomes the sacred duty of those who are in charge of the machinery of the government to suppress it and suppress it with an exemplary ruthlessness that will prevent the eventual shedding of rivers of blood.

I am about to show these plotters that the Republic of Turkey cannot be overthrown by murderers or through their murderous designs....

These left-overs from the former Young Turk Party, who should have been made to account for the lives of millions of our Christian subjects who were ruthlessly driven en masse, from their homes and massacred, have been restive under the Republican rule. They have hitherto lived on plunder, robbery and bribery and become inimical to any idea or suggestion to enlist in useful labor and earn their living by the honest sweat of their brow.

Under the cloak of the opposition party, this element, who forced our country into the Great War against the will of the people, who caused the shedding of rivers of blood of the Turkish youth to satisfy the criminal ambition of Enver Pasha, has, in a cowardly fashion, intrigued against my life, as well as the lives of the members of my cabinet. I would have more respect for them had they planned an armed revolution, taking the field in a manly fashion, to overthrow my government. But being conscious of the fact that they could not muster out even one regiment to give battle to the zealous adherents to, an [sic] upholders of, the glorious republic, they have resorted to bestial methods of assassination. They have hired murderers and even debauched women to commit their murderous acts.

In the middle of June last I had planned to make a tour of the country. My itinerary was published. A group of these assassins, placed on the route of procession, were to "rain" hand grenades at the automobiles which were to carry me and my staff.

WOMAN AS BOMBER

They went even further and seduced a woman who had been for years identified with my cause and who had been my loyal political friend and on occasions an adviser. They induced this woman to accept the reprehensible assignment to present me with a bouquet which concealed a bomb that would, on my receiving it, explode and obliterate everyone in sight. This ill-advised woman deserves pity, for she was made to believe that she would thus sacrifice her own life for the good of the fatherland. I was the enemy of the nation. She will be forgiven for her part in the plot, for she conscience-stricken, confessed to the proper authorities in time for me to cancel my intended tour.

Los Angeles Examiner, Sunday, August 1, 1926 (Sunday Edition, Section VI)

With the transcript as reference point, it is intended to examine the main criticisms Ataöv deploys to challenge the authenticity of the interview. Ataöv, writes in another paper on the approach academics should employ when examining theories.

> Falsifiability is a criterion in scholarship. All theories should be checked for correctness. All existing literature relevant to a problem have to be located and analyzed, and when sufficient new clues are obtained, the validity of former generalizations have to be re-tested. There is no need to cling to the original lopsided hypotheses. Scholarship is like a building in perpetual repair. Perpetuating the existing set of beliefs is not necessarily a scientific approach.[1]

It is in this spirit that existing literature will be re-examined and the 'fabrication hypotheses' levelled by Ataöv evaluated.

****

The Worldwide News Service: Armenian Fabrication or Fact?

At the foot of the Hildebrand interview published by the *Los Angeles Examiner*, there is a reference to the copyright belonging to "World-Wide News Service, Inc. of Boston". Ataöv suggests the location is significant given that Boston "happens to have the second largest concentration of Armenians in the United States." In Ataöv's view the Boston and Los Angeles connection, "immediately brings to mind a plot to serve an interest…"[2]

Contemporary accounts establish that Boston (along with New York and Los Angeles) did indeed host "assemblages" of the Armenian diaspora, but this in itself is not suspicious.[3] The location of a news syndicate in Boston is not exceptional, but rather entirely consistent

---

1 Ataöv, pp. 122-23.
2 Ataöv, p. 56.
3 Malcolm Vartan Malcom, *The Armenians in America* (Pilgrim Press, 1910), p. 73. Peter R Eisenstadt, *The Encyclopedia of New York State* (Syracuse University Press, 2005), p. 118.

The Los Angeles Examiner, 1st August 1926.

with the city's historic role as a US news hub.[1] *The Encyclopaedia of American Journalism*, cited by Ataöv, states that Boston published the first ever US newspaper and the first regular newspaper.[2] The introduction of transatlantic cables to Halifax, Nova Scotia in the mid-nineteenth century allowed Boston to exploit its geographical proximity to the Canadian telegraphic terminus and continue competing with other more easterly seaboard cities to maintain a news service.[3] This advantage did not last and by the late 1920s agencies began to shift to New York.[4] In 1926 it was entirely plausible, indeed likely, that a news agency would be based in Boston due to these historical factors and in itself is not indicative of an Armenian diaspora contrivance.

What of the Los Angeles location of the newspaper carrying the interview? Ataöv notes that the article "was printed in the State of California," and again concludes this is highly suspicious because of the area's large Armenian community.[5] The article was published by the *Los Angeles Examiner*, one of the extensive stable of newspaper titles owned by the press-magnate Randolph Hearst[6]. The Hildebrand interview appeared as syndicated copy in at least one other Hearst newspaper: the Texas based *San Antonio Light* on the same date. The

1 Richard Allen Schwarzlose, *The Nation's Newsbrokers: The Formative Years, from Pretelegraph to 1865*, vol. 1 (Northwestern University Press, 1989), p. 15.

2 Donald Paneth, *The Encyclopedia of American Journalism* (Fact of File Publications, 1983), pp. vii & viii.

3 David Halberstam, *Breaking News: How the Associated Press Has Covered War, Peace, and Everything Else* (Princeton Architectural Press, 2007), p. 405.

4 Martin Shefter, *Capital of the American Century: The National and International Influence of New York City* (Russell Sage Foundation, 1993), pp. 117-19.

5 Ataöv, p. 56.

6 Online Archive of California, "Hearst Corporation Los Angeles Examiner Photographs, Negatives and Clippings–Portrait Files (N-Z) 7000.1c, Background," (California: University of Southern California).

San Antonio Light, 15. August, 1926.

copy and accreditation remained the same, but the *San Antonio Light* sub-editor had changed the headline to read, "'I'll hang every plotter against Turkey's peace!' Warns Kemal." The by-line reads, "Only the misguided woman who confessed her part to conspiracy in time to save dictator's life will be forgiven, he says."[1]

Ataöv's allegations of a plot rely on his assertion that the interview originated from an agency located in a city (Boston) with a large Armenian diaspora and was restricted to publication in a city with a large diaspora (Los Angeles). For Ataöv's premise to hold good, there would need to be evidence that San Antonio was also an Armenian focal point. However, there is an absence of any such Armenian diaspora in San Antonio either in 1926 or indeed now. Detailed research on the distribution of the Armenian diaspora by Mark Aslan reveals there was no appreciable Armenian presence in San Antonio or Texas.[2] The 1916 US Census data documenting the distribution of Armenian Orthodox churches validates Aslan's research.[3] Of course, it could still be argued that a fictitious press agency concocted the interview, and succeeded in duping the *Los Angeles Examiner* and other

1 Karl Emil Hildebrand, "San Antonio Light," *'I'll hang every plotter against Turkey's peace!' Warns Kemal.",* 15 August 1926.

2 Mark B. Arslan, "Armenian Immigration Project," Shiplists, http://arslanmb.org/ArmenianImmigrants/shiplists.html#Findings. Accessed 2/2/2016

3 Sam L Rogers, "Religious Bodies 1916, Part 2. Seperate Denominations: History, Description & Statistics.," (Washington: US Dept of Commerce, Bureau of the Census, 1916).

Hearst papers to run it. To determine the likelihood of such a conclusion, the agency in question requires further scrutiny.

Did the Worldwide News Service (WNS) exist? Ataöv consults the *Encyclopaedia of American Journalism* and finds no reference to a WNS and suggests this is further proof of a 'plot.'[1] However, the Encyclopaedia makes no claim to be a comprehensive listing of all historic US journalistic ventures. A couple of significant omissions illustrate the point. The Encyclopaedia does not include various Hearst newspapers and operations. For example Hearst's *International News Service* and the *Los Angeles Examiner* is not included along with many other US newspapers. Put simply, the failure to include an entry for an organisation or periodical is not proof it did not exist. The publishers of Ataöv's own book, 'Okey Enterprises,' does not appear in the current American list of book publishers in the Publisher's Global database although it clearly exists.[2]

In fact a more rigorous search beyond one encyclopaedia establishes the existence of the WNS. A book by Judith Banki commemorating the work of the Human Rights activist, the late Rabbi Marc Tannebaum, mentions WNS as a regular disseminator of his work.[3] Another example is an article on dancing is cited in the 2012 'Dance Chronicle,' a Taylor and Francis published journal. The footnote reads, "*Spirituality in Dancing,*" World-Wide News Service, Inc., Boston, Mass., 1924, Anna Pavlova, scrapbooks, SFMPD.*[4]

There are also numerous references to the WNS in the *Southern Israelite*, a weekly paper published in Atlanta, Georgia and now archived in the University State System of Georgia, USA, where the

---

1 Ataöv, pp. 56-57.
2 Publishers Global, "United States: List of American Publishers," *Publishers Global* (USA: PublishersGlobal 2017).
3 Judith Herschcopf Banki and John Pawlikowski, *Ethics in the Shadow of the Holocaust: Christian and Jewish Perspectives* (Rowman & Littlefield, 2001), p. xvi.
4 Carrie Gaiser Casey, "The Ballet Corporealities of Anna Pavlova and Albertina Rasch," *Dance Chronicle* 35, no. 1 (2012): Footnote 23.

WNS is credited as the supplier of syndicated news stories.[1] The April 1937 edition of the *Southern Israelite* has WNS articles with a Middle Eastern/Jewish interest on the majority of its pages. The front page contains two WNS syndicated items: a lead item, and another article headed "Liquidation of Birobidjan plans denied by Soviet." The by-line reads, "Interview by Seven Arts Editor brings light on questionable status." The article provides further information about the interviewer, Joseph Brainin who is described as, "editor of the Seven Arts Feature syndicate and the Worldwide News Service."[2]

Various obituaries show Brainin founded the *Seven Arts Feature Syndicate* in 1921 and retired as its editor and managing director in 1938.[3] The University of Massachusetts Amherst retains an original letter written by Brainin in January 1931. The headed notepaper is topped by the imprint 'Seven Arts Feature Syndicate' and tailed with the legend, 'Exclusive Distributors of Worldwide News Service.'[4]

1 University System of Georgia, "The Southern Israelite Archive," in *GALILEO Scholar* (Georgia: Board of Regents of the University System of Georgia, 2017).

2 Worldwide News Syndicate, "Liquidation of Birobidjan Plans Denied by Soviet: Interview by Seven Arts Editor Burings Light on Questionable Status," *The Southern Israelite* 1937. http://newspapers-pdf.galileo.usg.edu/asi/asi1937/asi1937-0099.pdf. Accessed 10/2/2018

3 Death Announcement, "Joseph Brainin, Journalist and Associated with Weizmann Institute, Dies at 74," *Jewish Telegraphic Agency*, 9th February 1970, https://www.jta.org/1970/02/09/archive/joseph-brainin-journalist-and-associated-with-weizmann-institute-dies-at-74 Accessed 10/2/2018; Obituary, "Joseph Brainin Is Dead at 74; Aide of Weizmann Institute," *New York Times* 1970, https://www.nytimes.com/1970/02/09/archives/joseph-brainin-is-dead-at-74-aide-of-weizmann-institute.html Accessed 10/2/2018.

4 Joseph Brainin, "Letter from Seven Arts Feature Syndicate to Herbert J. Seligmann,," in *W. E. B. Du Bois Papers* ed. Seven Arts Feature Syndicate/Worldwide News Service (New York: Special Collections and University Archives, University of Massachusetts Amherst Libraries, 1931). http://credo.library.umass.edu/view/pageturn/mums312-b060-i466/#page/1/mode/1up. Accessed 01/2/2018

Additional research reveals references to The Seven Arts Feature Syndicate as "a news agency specialising in items of interest to the Jewish press."[1] The American Jewish Periodical Centre lists the Seven Arts Feature Syndicate with the alternative trading name of Worldwide News Service and (by then) operating from New York.[2] Further confirmation of the symbiotic linkage between Seven Arts Feature Syndicate and Worldwide News is referred to in the obituary of Brainin's successor named as the "editor of the Seven Arts Feature Syndicate and Worldwide News Service."[3]

Aside from the references cited above, there are further examples of Seven Arts Feature Syndicate/WNS syndicated stories appearing in North American media outlets. The earliest example uncovered pre-dates the 1926 Hildebrand interview and features a syndicated article in the Canadian *Jewish Chronicle* written in 1925.[4]

A Minor Newspaper in a Far Corner of the World?

Ataöv appears keen to relegate the status of the *Los Angeles Examiner* and thereby diminish its credentials. It was, he says, "a minor newspaper" but this is surely debatable; compared to what? It was founded by the newspaper magnate Randolph Hearst as his sixth newspaper and was a serious player in the southern California area. In 1925 the paper had a circulation of around 167,935, putting it ahead of its rival the *LA Times*.[5] Indeed, at the peak of its success it was the

1 Abraham Moses Klein, *Am Klein: The Letters* (University of Toronto Press, 2011), p. 346.

2 American Jewish Periodical Center, "Worldwide News Service & Seven Arts Feature Syndicate News," in *AJPC* (New York: Hebrew Union College/ Jewish Institute of Religion, 2017), p. 70.

3 Obituary, "Bernard Postal Dead at 75," *Jewish Telegraphic Agency*, 9th March 1981, https://www.jta.org/1981/03/09/archive/bernard-postal-dead-at-75 Accessed 01/2/2018

4 Hakim Ivan, "Is Palestine in Danger?," *The Canadian Jewish Chronicle*, 27th November 1925, p. 3.

5 See Rob Leicester Wagner, *Red Ink, White Lies: The Rise and Fall of Los Angeles Newspapers, 1920-1962* (Dragonflyer Press, 2000).

United States' largest circulation afternoon paper with a readership of 700,000 before suffering a significant decline in 1967 and closing in 1989.[1] Commensurate with its high status and aspirations the newspaper was located in a grand purpose-built headquarters that Hearst commissioned in 1913. Hearst instructed the architect that the building was to be

> ...the best equipped and largest building in the world devoted exclusively to the production of a newspaper; that it should be a worthy and substantial addition to the rapidly expanding business heart of Los Angeles.[2]

The building was completed in 1915 and lived up to Hearst's instructions: two storeys high and finished in an opulent Spanish Renaissance style featuring carved wood panels, hand painted floors, marble and gold. The multi-millionaire magnate maintained an apartment within the building from which he oversaw business.[3] Today the building is still owned by the Hearst Corporation and listed as a designated Los Angeles Cultural Monument.[4]

The newspaper went on to break a number of important stories including the most infamous "Black Dahlia" murder case in the 1940s. The story was fictionalised by the American crime writer,

1 See: Dave McNary, Memories of L.A. Herald-Examiner fading. 31 October 1990. https://www.upi.com/Archives/1990/10/31/Memories-of-LA-Herald-Examiner-fading/7068657349200/. Accessed 10/2/2018

2 See the official "A History of Our Building" reproduced on http://www.herald-examiner-los-angeles-filming-location.com/wp-content/uploads/Pages/About/img009.jpg Accessed 10/1/2018

3 See: Dave McNary, Memories of L.A. Herald-Examiner fading. 31 October 1990. https://www.upi.com/Archives/1990/10/31/Memories-of-LA-Herald-Examiner-fading/7068657349200/. Accessed 10/2/2018

4 See the Pacific Coast Architecture Database. Accessed 10/12/2018. http://pcad.lib.washington.edu/building/198/ and The Los Angeles City database for the historicalhttp://cityplanning.lacity.org/complan/HCM/dsp_hcm_result.cfm?community=Central%20City. Accessed 10/12/2018

James Ellroy in 1987 and became a 2006 Hollywood movie starring Scarlett Johansson.[1]

Aside from Ataöv's comments about the newspaper being minor, perhaps even more peculiar is his dismissive statement that the newspaper was printed in Los Angeles, "a far away corner of the world." This surely must constitute an interesting example of what might be termed "inverted" cognitive geography in which the viewer's perspective is distorted by their standpoint. Perhaps the best example is the (apocryphal) newspaper headline "Fog In Channel, Continent Cut Off" to illustrate skewed British perceptions of their geographical position. By no stretch of the imagination could 1926 Los Angeles be construed as a "corner of the world" in contrast to 1926 Ankara. The Californian economy underwent a massive expansion in the early 1920s fuelled by oil, banking and commerce, drawing in thousands of immigrants and becoming a modern, thriving, sprawling metropolis.[2] In addition Hollywood had already established itself as the global leader of entertainment creating the phenomena of movie celebrities.[3] Turkey in comparison experienced a wretched time. It was recovering from the chaos wrought by World War and the aftermath of the War of Independence, a fight for survival that had caused great destruction, emigration and the decimation of its merchant class. The experience strengthened Mustafa Kemal's resolve to rebuild and restructure the Republic that included the creation of a new capital in inland

1 For a general background into the media treatment of the Black Dahlia Murder case see: http://crimefeed.com/2017/01/the-black-dahlia-in-popular-culture-books-movies-music-more/. Accessed 10/2/2018

2 See Tom Sitton, *Metropolis in the Making: Los Angeles in the 1920s* (Univ of California Press, 2001) or Martin Wachs, "Autos, Transit, and the Sprawl of Los Angeles: The 1920s," *Journal of the American Planning Association* 50, no. 3 (1984).

3 For a history of the Hollywood movie industry see Jonathan D Silver, "Hollywood's Dominance of the Movie Industry: How Did It Arise and How Has It Been Maintained?" (Queensland University of Technology, 2007). https://eprints.qut.edu.au/16687/1/Jonathan_Derek_Silver_Thesis.pdf

Anatolia. The modern Ankara today is a tribute to Mustafa Kemal's vision; in 1926 it had hardly begun its transformation from provincial town to today's proud, modern capital city. It was described in these terms:

> In general, it very much resembles the popular idea of an American mining camp which has just struck oil. There are six or seven respectable buildings in a slightly Teutonic style of architecture – the Parliament House, the club and office of the 'People's Party,' the Soviet Embassy, the Secondary School and certain public offices – and a score or so of distempered modern houses, in one of which the American delegation is lodged: but except for a certain Eastern aspect, and a liberal use of mud in their construction the rest might be called shacks, and the best are hastily improvised two-storied buildings built in and out of the few Turkish houses that stand on the site. One enters the offices of even high officials through stable yards littered with manure, and passes up creaking outside wooden staircases into tiny dilapidated rooms. The discomforts of this place must be seen to be realised.

This description is confirmed by Kinross who describes 1920s Ankara as lacking basic infrastructure and suitable buildings for state departments and diplomatic missions. At this point it is worth highlighting the significance of the small town nature on Mustafa Kemal's socialising. Ankara was limited to a handful restaurants and hotels with the consequence that social activity centred on a few locations. Kinross names the Anatolian Club as a favourite haunt of Mustafa Kemal. It was here he indulged in late night pastimes such as card playing and dancing. Since the club was small it allowed "it's few foreign habitués to meet at close quarters..."[1] The willingness of Mustafa Kemal to frequent public places and engage with foreigners

---

1 Patrick Kinross, *Ataturk*, Hachette UK, 2012. pp. 406-407.

he found of interest is a matter of some significance and will be returned to later in the context of his stay in Izmir 1926.

Another pertinent question that requires addressing is, why would a Los Angeles readership be bothered with news from a far away corner of the world (Turkey)? The answer might surely be because Los Angeles featured a significant Armenian émigré population to which a Hearst newspaper might want to appeal. In addition, was it not possible a wider Los Angeles readership might also have had some interest in events in far away Turkey? After all the US populace had been subjected to a sustained stream of sensational and lurid descriptions of the fate of the Armenians just a few years earlier. These had appeared in the form of propagandising newspaper reports and in a book by the former US Ambassador to the Ottoman Empire, Henry Morgenthau.[1] Karpat refers to a period of "… endless tales of oppression, injustice and maltreatment," by the Ottomans, "aimed primarily at arousing… sympathy and support." These stories had appeared "in the press of the United States and elsewhere, often backed up by reports of missionaries or local priests."[2] Mustafa Kemal's motive in hoping to reach a US audience can be seen in this context: an attempt to tap US public prejudices so judiciously fanned against the Ottomans in the recent past. A message crafted to maximise support for the new Turkey and his actions in bringing to justice the very people accountable for the massacres; the remnants of the CUP.

There remains one further question: why would the Hearst newspaper empire use stories from a relatively small wire service specialising in Jewish and Middle Eastern interests in preference to their own 'International News Service' (INS) operation? The answer lies in the rivalry between Hearst and his mainstream competitors. The Associated Press (AP) established a virtual monopoly on the flow

---

1 Henry Morgenthau, *Ambassador Morgenthau's Story* (London: Gomidas Institute, 2016).
2 Karpat, Kemal H. "The Ottoman Emigration to America, 1860–1914." *International Journal of Middle East Studies* 17, no. 02 (1985): pp. 175-209.

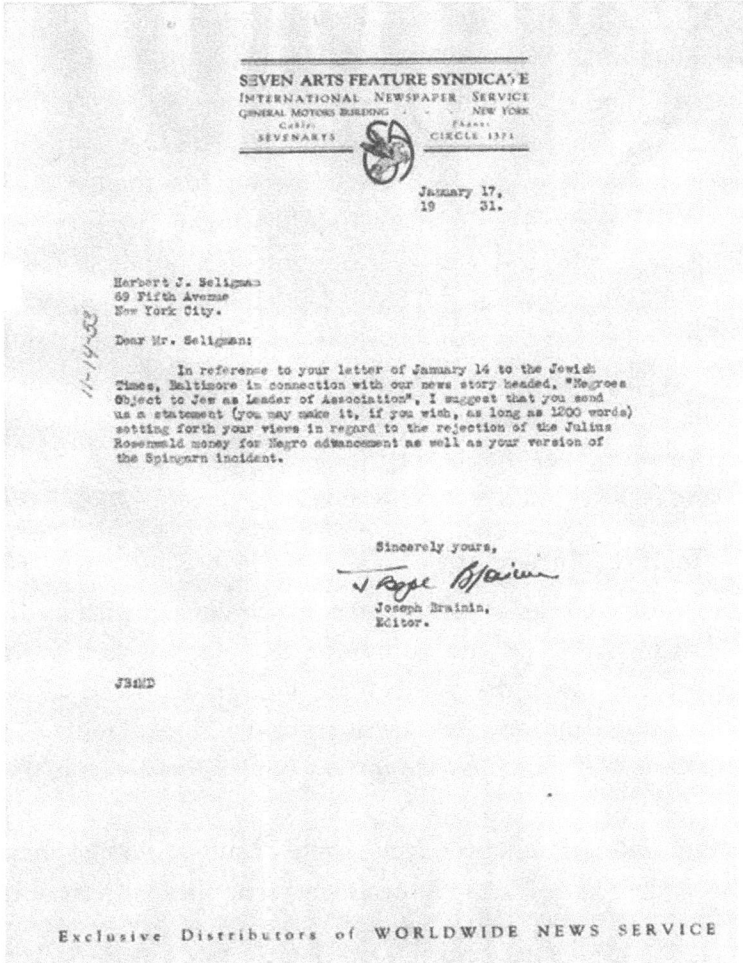

SEVEN ARTS FEATURE SYNDICATE
INTERNATIONAL NEWSPAPER SERVICE
GENERAL MOTORS BUILDING · · NEW YORK
Cable: *Phone:*
SEVENARTS CIRCLE 1371

January 17,
19 31.

Herbert J. Seligman
69 Fifth Avenue
New York City.

Dear Mr. Seligman:

In reference to your letter of January 14 to the Jewish
Times, Baltimore in connection with our news story headed, "Negroes
Object to Jew as Leader of Association", I suggest that you send
us a statement (you may make it, if you wish, as long as 1200 words)
setting forth your views in regard to the rejection of the Julius
Rosenwald money for Negro advancement as well as your version of
the Spingarn incident.

Sincerely yours,

Joseph Brainin

Joseph Brainin,
Editor.

JB:MD

Exclusive Distributors of WORLDWIDE NEWS SERVICE

Reproduced here with permission from Special Collections
& University Archives, UMass Amherst Libraries.

of foreign news into the US, obtaining exclusive arrangements with the three dominant European news agencies: Reuters in Great Britain, Havas in France, and Wolff in Germany.[1] In the early 1900s AP excluded the Hearst news empire forcing Hearst to establish INS as means of securing foreign news. The attempt was not completely successful. During World War I, his papers' pro-German stance alienated foreign wires services to the extent the British, French, Portuguese and Japanese agencies excluded Hearst's INS from all their news services.[2] This left INS so desperate for foreign news it plagiarised AP copy. This resulted in AP bringing a court case for breach of copyright and was heard by the US Supreme Court in December 1918.[3] Although AP failed to establish copyright on actual news, the Court decided that specific stories about events should be regarded as copyright. Thus INS was forced to develop its own alternative means of collating and distributing foreign news items.[4] It is in this context that the use of the Seven Arts Features Syndicate's Worldwide News is likely to have occurred.

The Style of the Interview

In his opening comments Ataöv points up an apparent contradiction in the article: who was the author of the piece? The *Los Angeles Examiner* piece states the words, "are written by Mustafa Kemal Pasha," but was also, "an interview with Emile Hildebrand…" Ataöv believes this is contradictory: it must be one or the other. Is this the case?

It is important to acknowledge the role of sub-editors in preparing an article. Their function is to furnish news articles with heads, sub-

---

1 Marlene Cuthbert, "Reaction to International News Agencies: 1930s and 1970s Compared," *Gazette (Leiden, Netherlands)* 26, no. 2 (1980): p. 101.

2 Christopher H. Sterling, *Encyclopedia of Journalism*, 6 vols., vol. 1 (Thousand Oaks, California: SAGE Publications Inc, 2009), p. 775.

3 US Supreme Court, "International News Service V. Associated Press, 248 U.S. 215 (1918)," in *No 231*, ed. US Supreme Court (Washington DC1918).

4 Sterling, 1, p. 775.

headings and acknowledgements regarding the author or correspondent. Working under pressure against deadlines, they may not always be accurate. The issues of accuracy associated with headlines and other information not inserted by the article's author are not the fault of the journalist since they, "would almost certainly written by a sub-editor…"[1]

What of the style of article itself that appears to be an impromptu interview and relies on verbatim reporting of the interviewee's words? The Carnegie Mellon University Libraries contain digitalised archives of a Jewish newspaper published in Pittsburgh and these contain an insight into journalistic practices and the ability to approach and interview important persons in a way that is less likely today. In 1931 the *Jewish Criterion* published two syndicated articles relating to an interview with the NSDAP leader Adolf Hitler. The interviewee was Max Fraenkel, the Seven Arts Feature Syndicate/WNS Berlin correspondent who obtained an unofficial and unauthorised interview whilst Hitler dined in a restaurant. The journalist ignored bodyguards and approached Hitler as he dined in the restaurant. Despite there being no appointment, Hitler agreed to a short, impromptu interview that was subsequently published in the US. Putting aside the obvious difference in content and the nature of the subject aside, the interview is notable in its similarity to the method and style of the alleged Hildebrand interview, namely its unofficial nature but perhaps more significantly the manner in which the interview was written up; the subject is quoted at length and verbatim.[2] Indeed, it was reported that Hitler was angry with the verbatim style of the written up article, not the accuracy:

> Hitler, not denying the authenticity of the views expressed, is upset because he did not realise that his ideas would be

1 Cribb, Julian, and Tjempaka Sari. *Open Science: Sharing Knowledge in the Global Century*, CSIRO Publishing, 2010. p. 78.
2 Max Fraenkel, "Adolf Hitler Explains, an Exclusive Interview with Germany's Fascist Chieftain," *The Jewish Criterion*, 23rd January 1931, 3. See online Collection of Carnegie Mellon University for copy.

put between quotation marks. He thought he was to be quoted indirectly.[1]

The pertinent point here is the fact that the Hitler/Fraenkel interview contained large tranches of verbatim quotes by the 1920s interviewee (Hitler) and written up by the interviewer (Fraenkel). As such Hitler was the 'author' of his own words and Fraenkel the author of the article. Ataöv characterises the *Los Angeles Examiner* article as claiming to be "written by" Mustafa Kemal, but it makes no such claim. Instead, the article claims to be the words uttered "by Mustafa Kemal Pasha," as recorded by the journalist and recorded verbatim. It is disingenuous to claim otherwise.

The matter of the office location of *Seven Arts Feature Syndicates* needs addressing to allay any concerns this might be unusual and excite a conspiracy theory. It is evident that Joseph Brainin relocated his operations from Boston to New York sometime in the late 1920s. In doing so he was following a pattern of behaviour exhibited by other larger news and media operations as previously mentioned. It was not unusual for news services agencies to take advantage of differing state laws in respect of taxation and fiduciary requirements. Thus a company may be domiciled in one state, but operate in another, or may choose to dissolve and restart in another location. As a case in point *Associated Press* (AP) did precisely this on a number of occasions in the 1920s. For example, at one point AP was operating from New York but incorporated in Chicago, then, upon losing a case in the Illinois Supreme Court, dissolved itself and reincorporated in New York to take advantage of laxer incorporation laws.[2]

---

1 "Hitler Angry at Interview on Jews.," *The Jewish Criterion*, 6th February 1931, 10. See online Collection of Carnegie Mellon University for copy.
2 Margaret A Blanchard, *Revolutionary Sparks: Freedom of Expression in Modern America* (Oxford University Press, 1992), p. 29.
Bill Kovarik, *Revolutions in Communication: Media History from Gutenberg to the Digital Age* (Bloomsbury Publishing USA, 2015), p. 187.

Karl Emile Hildebrand: "Did Anyone By That Name Ever Live?"

Having addressed the antecedents of the WNS and the reasons why Hearst newspapers ran syndicated WNS articles, there remains the issue of the Swiss journalist. Ataöv entered into extensive correspondence with Swiss authorities, journals, and a family bearing such a name. Ataöv declares himself unable "to produce any evidence" that a person of that name "or approximate spellings" ever "lived in and around 1926." He concludes the absence of such a person is "definitive evidence" of falsification.[1] He asks, "did anyone by that name ever live?"[2]

A person with "that approximate" spelling did live around 1926. Aside from the missing 'e' in 'Emile' the name is identical: Karl Emil Hildebrand. At a stroke, Ataöv's 'definitive evidence' statement is undermined. Or perhaps not… is this Hildebrand: a person of a journalistic background and of the right age in 1926 to have conducted an interview?

The Hildebrand in question was a Swedish journalist, politician and academic. Hildebrand is listed in the online Swedish National Biography listings of prominent Swedes maintained by the National Archives of Sweden and is revealed to have lived from 1870 to 1952.[3] This would have made Hildebrand fifty-six at the time of the interview. Hildebrand worked for the *Stockholms Dagblad,* a centre-right inclined newspaper.[4] Employed first as a journalist, he served as the newspaper's Chief Editor from 1904 to 1913.[5] Stockholm City archives retain a

---

1 Ataöv, p. 61.
2 Ibid., p. 67.
3 Rikarkivet, "Karl E H Hildebrand," Riksarkivet, the National Archives of Sweden, https://sok.riksarkivet.se/Sbl/Presentation.aspx?id=13587#Meriter. Accessed 2/2/2016.
4 Karl Erik Gustafsson and Per Rydén, *A History of the Press in Sweden* (Nordicom, 2010), p. 201.
5 Herman Hofberg, *Svenskt Biografiskt Handlexikon (Swedish Biographical Handbook)*, ed. Digitalised on Project Runeberg (Stockholm: Albert Bonniers Forlag, 1909), p. 806.

Karl Emil Hildebrand (1870-1952),
Swedish journalist and academic.

January 1913 promotional film of the *Stockholms Dagblad* that includes footage of Hildebrand at his desk signing off copy as Chief Editor.[1]

Is it possible that the news agency or the Hearst newspaper subeditor mixed up the nationality of Hildebrand? Confusing Sweden with Switzerland is a historic and on-going occurrence. A cursory examination of print and social media reveals the mixing of the two states to be a persistent problem and not just in English speaking US, but also among Chinese, Russian, and Spanish speakers across the globe. A likely reason is the similarity in the names of the two countries in a number of languages. In Turkish, the names are *İsviçre* (Switzerland) and *İsveç* (Sweden).

This confusion/conflation phenomenon has spawned *YouTube* and blog comments from Swedes experiencing multiple instances of Americans conflating the two countries.[2] Similar experiences have been posted by Swiss residents in Canada.[3] In 2015 the University of Arkansas hosted some exchange students and took them to meet US

---

1 Stockholms Dagblad, "Stockholms Dagblad Hq," (Stocholms Stad, 1913). See Frames 1:39 to 2.07 https://stockholmskallan.stockholm.se/post/ 29716 Accessed 10/02/2018.

2 "Sweden vs Switzerland." Student Blogs from the Karolinska Institutet. Accessed 3/2/2017. https://studentblogski.wordpress.com/2014/01/27/ sweden-vs-switzerland/Gardefjord, Adam. Elevator talk, coffee, and naked guys: a swede in San Francisco. Weldon Owen Blog, 27/11/2012. Accessed 2/2/2017. http://www.weldonowen.com/blog/elevator-talk-coffee-and-nak ed-guys-swede-san-francisco?fb_coment_id=530900630254899_6496538#f 228 890c38; Joline, "Sweden not Switzerland: Some Help for Confused Americans..." Joline Blog, 3/7/2006, Accessed 2/2/2017; Hartvig, Yasmine. Sweden is not Switzerland. Accessed 3/2/2017. https://www.youtube.com/ watch?v =GOSBspyb3II. TASIS The American School In Switzerland: Switzerland, Not Sweden. 10/2/2016. Accessed 2/2/2017. https:// www.youtube.com/watch?v=eblV9AMuZ8E.

3 Marina, Switzerland vs Sweden: 2 different countries – 2 different languages. EC Vancouver Blog. 9/8/2012. Accessed 2/2/2016. http:// www.ecenglish.com/en/social/blog/vancouver/2012/08/09/switzerland-vs- sweden-2-different-countries-2-different-languages.

students. "Several confused Sweden with Switzerland so we talked about that. Some asked us what language we speak, and we explained about Swedish."[1] An Indian student in Sweden experienced the same conflation of Switzerland and Sweden from his Indian friends and family.[2]

Nor is this confusion restricted to the general public. Ron Suskind, the former senior national-affairs reporter for *The Wall Street Journal* recounts precisely such a mistake made by President George W. Bush in discussions with cross party representatives discussing the Israeli-Palestine road map. Congressman Tom Lantos suggested Sweden's 25,000 strong army might be the ideal candidate to form a peacekeeping force. Bush confused the two countries and dismissed the suggestion as impossible, stating Sweden had no standing army. Later Bush acknowledged his error.[3]

In 1991 President Ronald Reagan addressing the Swedish-American Business Club announced his wish to visit Stockholm on his next visit to 'Switzerland'. Yale Professor George C. Schoolfield comments, "the inadvertency showed, once again, how closely the Great Communicator was in touch with the American spirit: the mix-up is a common one. The two names are easily confused, primarily [because] they sound alike..." Schoolfield goes on to say, "both [countries] are neutral, spared from war over the last two centuries, both are highly developed welfare states and so forth."[4]

---

1 Students from Australia, Sweden Teach and Learn in Fayetteville School, Nov. 20, 2015. Accessed 3/2/2016. http://news.uark.edu/articles/33025/students-from-australia-sweden-teach-and-learn-in-fayetteville-school.
2 Koran, Prasanth. P.S: Sweden is not Switzerland, Blog, 5/1/2015. Accessed 3/2/2016. https://www.kth.se/blogs/prasanth/tag/difference-between-sweden-and-swiss/
3 Ron Susskind, "Faith, Certainty and the Presidency of George W. Bush," *New York Times Magazine*, 17th October 2004.
4 George C Schoolfield, "Utopien Von Freiheit: Die Schweiz Im Spiegel Der Schwedischen Literatur. Beiträge Zur Nordischen Philologie 23," *Scandinavian Studies* 69, no. No 2 (1997): p. 259.

The mixing of the two countries is a global phenomenon. In China the confusion is so acute that the Swiss and Swedish governments launched a joint campaign in 2013 to facilitate the public's distinction of the two countries.[1] The issue has entered popular humour/culture with the Urban dictionary containing an entry for "Not Switzerland" with a claimed meaning: "Description of Sweden. Often used as a direct suffix to Sweden, since many Americans think that Sweden and Switzerland are the same country."[2] The Swedish crime writer Jan Arnald (pen name Arne Dahl) attended a book launch/discussion at Barnes & Noble, New York in 2012 and joked that he hoped the success of 'Scandi-noir' TV crime dramas might stop Sweden being confused with Switzerland.[3] It appears a somewhat forlorn hope. In 2016 an Australian sub-editor repeated the error. An online article headline referred to migrant attacks in *Sweden*, but the article related to incidents in Zurich, Switzerland.[4]

This last example provides an example that not even newspaper sub-editors are immune from the tendency of mixing up Swiss and Swede when crafting introductory text to accompany an accurate new story. Ninety years before the 2016 Australian sub-editor's mistake it is likely the same mistake occurred; a sub-editor mistakenly switched Hildebrand's nationality from Swedish to Swiss. The sub-editor appears to have compounded his error by conflating the journalist Karl Emil Hildebrand with the contemporaneous artist Ernst

1 Soo. Kim, "Chinese Confuse Sweden with Switzerland: Sweden and Switzerland Have Launched a Joint Awareness Campaign to Help Chinese Tourists Tell the Two Countries Apart.," *Daily Telegraph*, 12th November 2013.
2 See "Not Switzerland," Urban Dictionary, https://www.urbandiction ary.com/define.php?term=Not%20Switzerland. Accessed 10/2/2018.
3 Nordstjernan. Arne Dahl and the writing duo Anders Roslund and Börge Hellström at Barnes & Noble, New York in January, 2012. 4.0 mins to 4.07 mins. Accessed 2/2/2016. https://www.youtube.com/watch?v=xBtp8o4kGJ0.
4 News.com.au, "New Year's Eve Sex Assaults Also Reported in Finland, Sweden and Austria," (News Corp Australian Network, 2016).

Hildebrand whose work is recorded as having sold in the US. The artist Ernst Hildebrand had died in November 1924 and as such he would be still be recorded as living in any 'Who's Who' type reference work published pre June 1926 and consulted by the sub-editor. This would explain the sub-editor's decision to describe the composite Hildebrand as both a journalist and artist.[1]

Karl Emil Hildebrand and Travels to the Orient

Whilst establishing the existence of a person named Hildebrand in the correct time period, what evidence is there that the Swedish, journalist/academic Hildebrand had any business to be in Turkey?

In 1926 Hildebrand travelled through Europe to Asia to conduct field research for a book on China. *Det Gamla Och Det Nya Kina* was published in 1927.[2] It is impossible to prove beyond doubt Hildebrand's route to Shanghai, but it would have certainly involved a sea voyage through the Suez Canal, since an overland route would have been impractical. To reach Egypt the most direct and safest would be a combination of train and sea travel. This would have entailed travelling by train from Stockholm to Berlin and from there to Istanbul. A short ferry ride linked Istanbul to Bandırma, and the Smyrna-Cassaba Line to Izmir.[3] A French shipping company, the Messageries Maritimes offered passage from Izmir (Smyrna) on their

1 If there can be any further doubt about the ability to muddle an individual's national identity in the early twentieth century, the case of Ernst Hildebrand illustrates the issue. Ernst Hildebrand is sometimes described as German, Swedish and sometimes Swiss in current art auctions and catalogues. For description of nationality in art auctions see: https://www.invaluable.co.uk/artist/hildebrand-ernst-5mecgfwrxm/sold-at-auction-prices/. Accessed 10/2/2018.
2 Hildebrand Karl Emil, *Det Gamla Och Det Nya Kina (the Old and the New China.)* (Stockholm: Hugo Gebers Förlag, 1927).
3 See the specialist 'Trains of Turkey website' for details and a schematic map. http://www.trainsofturkey.com/pmwiki.php/History/SCP Accessed 2/2/2016

Mediterranean circular line north-south route to Alexandria.[1] The same company offered a train passage to Port Said and from there sea passage to Shanghai and other Chinese ports via the Suez Canal – a voyage of about thirty-four days.[2]

There is a documented Hildebrand association with Turkey. In 1927 he agreed to write the introduction for a Swedish translation of a book by a leading British political commentator J. A. Spender.[3] *Österns Förvandling* (The Changing East) was an account of Spender's travels to Turkey, Egypt and India.[4] Spender arrived in Turkey in December 1925 and stayed in Istanbul for a month, then visited Ankara before returning to Istanbul.[5] Is it possible Hildebrand travelling through to China, made his acquaintance with Spender on that journey in late 1925 and then, on his own return via Izmir, was granted an ad hoc interview with Mustafa Kemal in June 1926?

Ataöv believes the failure of the Turkish domestic press to cover Mustafa Kemal's remarks is further evidence of their forgery. This ignores the likelihood the Hildebrand interview was aimed at a foreign audience. The Turkish press was rigidly controlled and if a particular narrative or chain of events was deemed not suitable for a domestic audience, it was not published. Andrew Mango cites Fuat (Cebesoy) on the effect the 1925 'Maintenance of Order Law (Takrir-i-Sükûn Kanunu) had on the free press; "...the press was deprived of the right to criticise and control the government..."[6] The publication cited by

---

1 See the 1926 Messageries Maritimes Booklet and the ship listing complied by Björn Larsson on the Maritime Timetable Images website. http://www.timetableimages.com/maritime/images/mm.htm Accessed 2/2/2016.

2 Arndt Graf and Chua Beng Huat, *Port Cities in Asia and Europe* (Routledge, 2008), p. 20.

3 Gordon Martel, *The Month That Changed the World: July 1914* (Oxford: Oxford University Press (UK), 2014), p. 136.

4 John Alfred Spender, *Österns Förvandling* (Stockholm: Geber, 1927).

5 John Alfred Spender, *The Changing East* (Cassell and Company, Ltd., 1926), pp. 27-61.

6 Andrew Mango, *Atatürk: The Biography of the Founder of Modern Turkey* (2011), p. 426.

Ataöv, the *Hakimiyet-i-Milliye*, was founded by Mustafa Kemal himself and was therefore hardly likely to speak out of turn.[1] Indeed, Mango describes it as a "mouth piece" of the regime.[2] Zürcher refers to the government closing down all national and provincial reporting apart from two "state organs," the *Hakimiyet-i-Milliye* and Istanbul based *Cumhuriyet*.[3]

Even prior to the 1925 press clampdown, news was circumscribed and sometimes blacked out completely with no reference in official accounts. One pertinent example of 'controlled' news is the absence of any Turkish press record relating to an earlier attempted assassination of Mustafa Kemal on the 7th January 1924. The attempt occurred in the hallway of his Izmir holiday residence and only the dramatic intervention of Latife, Mustafa Kemal's wife, succeeded in diverting the assassin's grenade and ensured Mustafa Kemal was uninjured.[4] Ipek Çalışlar comments,

> Strangely missing from official records and memoirs is the assassination attempt in Izmir [1924], where Latife and Mustafa Kemal had gone in such good cheers and came to the brink of death. But it was widely reported in the international press.[5]

According to Çalışlar, the 1924 assassination attempt was confirmed by Latife's nephew, Mehmet Sadık Öke. How is the absence of the reported assassination in the domestic press to be explained? Either the incident did not happen and the Turkish authorities made it up or it was suppressed for the domestic audience. Çalışlar makes the point Turkish authorities clearly understood the value of spinning a news story for a foreign audience.[6] This view of the 1926 incident is

---

1   Stanford J Shaw, *Reform, Revolution, and Republic: The Rise of Modern Turkey 1808-1975* (Cambridge: Cambridge University Press, 1977), p. 347.
2   Mango, p. 420.
3   Erik J Zürcher, *Turkey: A Modern History* (IB Tauris, 2004), p. 172.
4   İpek Çalislar, *Madam Atatürk: The First Lady of Modern Turkey* (London: Saki Books, 2013), pp. 163-65.
5   Ibid., pp. 21-22.
6   Ibid.

endorsed by Zürcher, "…there can be serious doubt, however, about the authenticity and reliability of this text, and even if it was authentic, it was meant for foreign consumption."[1] This episode highlights a crucial aspect of the regime's distinction between domestic and foreign audiences and a willingness to produce different messages accordingly. Placing the Hildebrand interview in this context would see the article as an attempt to spin the imminent crackdown on opposition members as justified by tying it to the Armenian massacres. This was a line likely to evoke sympathy in a foreign audience and less likely to appeal to elements of Turkish domestic opinion. Could not Mustafa Kemal recognised that this chance meeting with a foreign journalist offered a conduit to a foreign readership?

Karl Emil Hildebrand's Background

How though would such a chance meeting come about? Would there have been sufficient motive for the Turkish president to want to engage with an obscure Swedish journalist in an unscheduled and unofficial meeting in the first place? In fact, Karl Emil Hildebrand was anything but an obscure journalist. Hildebrand was exactly the sort of individual likely to engage Mustafa Kemal's keen intellect. In addition to his journalistic activities Hildebrand was both an academic and public servant. Gaining a PhD in political history, he had continued academic studies during World War I conducting military field research in the war torn Austro-Hungarian Empire for his first book, *Dual Monarchy at War.*[2] Aside from these attributes, there was an array of different career positions Hildebrand had held of interest to a president seeking to fashion a modern, secular and secure Turkish republic. Hildebrand had served two terms as an MP in the *Andra Kammaren,* (1906-1908 and 1911-1918). Hildebrand served on two important state bodies: 'People's Food Commission,' the organisation

---

1 Zürcher, p. 314.
2 Karl Emil Hildebrand, *Johan Iii Och Europas Katolska Makter, 1568-1580: Studier I 1500-Talets Politiska Historia* (Stockholm: Almqvist & Wiksells boktryckeriaktiebolag, 1898).&565. Bernard Piotrowski, "Sweden and the Question of Poland's Independence (1914–1918)," (1992): p. 15.

tasked with alleviating Sweden's parlous food supplies in WWI, and after the War had been appointed Chairman of the Riksgäldsfullmäktig, the state institution charged with managing Sweden's National Debt.[1]

During the 1909 Swedish General Strike, as editor of the *Stockholms Dagblad*, a leading newspaper, he took a firm stand against the strikers. As a parliamentarian, Hildebrand attempted to pass legislation aimed at regulating secondary picketing, the so-called '*Lex Hildebrand*'. Turkey had experienced its own series of strikes in May 1924. Strikers defied a court ruling banning union agitation and stepped up their action throughout the summer. Mustafa Kemal had promised to instigate new labour laws.[2] The introduction of the Maintenance of Order Law, a response to the Şeyh Sait Revolt in 1925 postponed any progress on a labour law.[3] Here then is an explicit area of industrial relations Hildebrand's experience as a journalist and legislator of direct relevance to the very issues Mustafa Kemal was addressing. Nor was this the only area. Universal suffrage and female emancipation were integral to Mustafa Kemal's vision of a new Turkey. In Sweden Hildebrand had supported measures of a similar nature including the introduction of universal suffrage and proportional representation for elections to the *Andra Kammaren* (1904-1905).[4] Furthermore, he had written a book expounding the extension of democracy.[5] The *Stockholms Dagblad* was notable for employing a large number of female journalists under Hildebrand's editorship. Sweden finally achieved universal suffrage in 1921. In short,

1 Karl Emil Hildebrand, "Contributors Listing," in *The Encyclopedia Britannica* ed. Panel Editors (London: Encyclopedia Britannica 1922), p. xii. Rikarkivet.
2 Loren Goldner, "'Socialism in One Country' before Stalin, and the Origins of Reactionary 'Anti-Imperialism': The Case of Turkey, 1917–1925," *Critique* 38, no. 4 (2010): pp. 631-61.
3 Mango, p. 424.
4 Rikarkivet.
5 Ataöv, p. 55.

Hildebrand's curriculum vitae matched a variety of concerns and interests shared by the leader of a new state grappling with many similar issues not to mention a shared interest in military matters.

There is one other point that might account for Hildebrand's presence in Izmir. The person Mustafa Kemal charged with reforming Turkish Law was Mahmut Esat Bozkurt, the serving National Assembly Member for Izmir with an interest in both law and commerce. Bozkurt served both as Minister of Economy (1924 1925) and Minister of Justice (1926). German speaking (as was Hildebrand) Bozkurt (educated in Switzerland) had received petitions regarding the applicability of Swiss, Italian and Swedish laws.[1]

It is important to note too that that Mustafa Kemal would have had no any difficulty in conversing with Hildebrand as he too was fluent in German to the extent he had translated a number of military books from German into Turkish.[2]

Perhaps even more extraordinary was Hildebrand's other connection to Turkey; his son-in-law Carl Einar af Wirsén was the Chairman of the League of Nations Commission established to adjudicate on the Mosul question.[3] The latter was one of the many intractable disputes associated with the Sykes-Picot imposition of post Ottoman boundaries and Mosul, with its oil fields being of critical importance to Turkey. The Committee had adjudicated in Britain's favour, but further negotiations had resulted in the Treaty of Angora signed less than two

---

1 Umut Azak, *Islam and Secularism in Turkey: Kemalism, Religion and the Nation State* (IB Tauris, 2010), p. 10.
Charles Kurzman, *Modernist Islam, 1840-1940: A Sourcebook* (Oxford University Press, USA, 2002), p. 217.
2 Edward J Erickson, *Mustafa Kemal Atatürk* (Bloomsbury Publishing, 2013), pp. 60-61.
3 H Müller-Sommerfeld, "The League of Nations, a-Mandates and Minority Rights During the Mandate Period in Iraq," *PDF hosted at the Radboud Repository of the Radboud University Nijmegen* (2016): p. 272.
Linköping University, "Af Wirsén, Carl Einar Thure," *Project Runeberg* V W - Viroulet-Fagerström (2017): p. 984.

weeks earlier on June 5th, but with ratifications not complete until July 18th. The issue therefore remained 'live' in June 1926. Moreover, even the signed agreement required further discussion. First regarding the composition of a new commission to finalise border demarcations and secondly to ensure the implementation of oil revenue for Turkey to be administered correctly.[1] In summary, there were a whole host of reasons why a bored Mustafa Kemal might have sought to exploit the opportunity to meet-up with a passing, well-connected German-speaking Swedish academic.

Ataöv asserts that there are no official accounts of any such meeting or coverage of a Hildebrand 'interview.' This is not necessarily surprising on a number of counts. Firstly, Mustafa Kemal enjoyed a well-established reputation for seeking his own entertainment.[2] He habitually chose to break his routine by making impromptu detours from his official diarised schedule. Whilst dining at a hotel he might invite guests to his table and he was capable of going 'walkabout,' or embarking on ad hoc, nocturnal excursions. One such example is recorded by Andrew Mango. During a provincial tour of Konya, Mustafa Kemal decided to leave the venue of a luncheon and "took his friends as far as a local hotel."[3] On another occasion Mustafa Kemal informed his wife he was unable to sleep and desired a nocturnal tram ride. The arrangements were hastily made and Mustafa Kemal spent the night riding and driving a tram.[4]

Mustafa Kemal's habit of drinking and dining with foreign journalists and academics was a practice he shared with another reforming leader: Iran's Reza Shah.

---

1 Treaty between the UK and Iraq and Turkey. Treaty Series No. 18 (1927) See articles 3 & 11. The original treaty is available at: http://treaties.fco.gov.uk/docs/pdf/1927/TS0018.pdf
2 Erickson, p. 57. Mango, p. 215.
3 Andrew Mango, *Atatürk: The Biography of the founder of Modern Turkey*, p. 420.
4 Çalışlar, pp. 167-69.

Academics, writers and journalists were there to be used for a purpose - to feed the leaders with ideas (as during Atatürk's famous all-night drinking bouts, where the problems as well as the future of the country were constantly debated)...[1]

In the early days of his presidency, Mustafa Kemal relied on foreign intellectuals due to the absence of home grown intellectuals with knowledge of modern European institutions and ideas. Thus Mustafa Kemal's practice of inviting intellectual outsiders to his dinner table can be seen as an ad hoc attempt to emulate something akin to a think-tank discussion to learn new approaches and stimulate ideas. The impromptu practice of inviting guests to his dinner continued in later years and included discussions on "political and economic issues and revolutionary ideas."[2] One pertinent example of a stranger being invited over to his restaurant table is contained in the memoirs of a US poet who, whilst dining in an Ankara hotel was unexpectedly invited to sit at Mustafa Kemal's table with her colleague, a *New York Times* reporter, Gladys Baker. Mustafa Kemal spoke to Baker for the entire night.[3] Baker duly wired her unofficial interview which was published in the US and copyrighted.[4]

Having established that Mustafa Kemal was most certainly in the habit of engaging with visiting journalists and academics in an off the record situation, is it not possible that this is exactly what occurred with Hildebrand?

1 Erik J Zürcher and Touraj Atabaki, "Men of Order: Authoritarian Modernization under Ataturk and Reza Shah," (London: IB Tauris & Co, 2004), p. 10.

2 Vamik Volkan, *Blind Trust: Large Groups and Their Leaders in Times of Crisis and Terror* (Pitchstone Publishing (US&CA), 2014), Chap 7.

3 Sara Henderson Hay, *Seasons of the Heart, in Quest of Faith: Poems by Sara Henderson Hay*, ed. Dikran Y Hadidian, Princeton Theological Monograph Series (Eugene, Oregon: Pickwick Publications, 1989), p. 8.

4 Library of Congress (US), "Catalog of Copyright Entries. Part 1. Group 2," 32, no. Nos 1-12 (1935): p. 510.

An Opportunity to Meet Hildebrand

Do timelines and circumstances allow for a meeting between Mustafa Kemal and Hildebrand in Izmir on the 22nd June 1926, the date of the supposed interview? The short answer is, yes. In the aftermath of the assassination attempt, Mustafa Kemal began a prolonged stay in Izmir. As Ataöv states, Mustafa Kemal summoned the failed assassin Ziya Hurşit to his hotel for a personal interrogation.[1] He also instructed Prime Minister İnönü to send the Independence Tribunal to Izmir by special train immediately.[2] Their arrival in Izmir on the 18th June 1926 coincided with the first official announcement of the assassination plot.[3]

Between June 18th and June 25th the Independence Tribunal focussed on preparing the indictments.[4] Mustafa Kemal remained in his Izmir hotel and keen to effect an air of normality he engaged in social and leisurely pursuits including attendance at a tennis match and a football match.[5] In these circumstances of enforced inactivity, it is possible Mustafa Kemal met Hildebrand and granted him an interview. Ataöv's examination of the records of *Hakimiyet-i-Milliye* newspaper reveals no such interview ever appeared in print; "had the interview taken place on the 22nd June, it would have appeared in the 26th June issue of the paper."[6] The significance of Ataöv's revelation of a domestic news blackout appears lost on him. There was no coverage of any of Mustafa Kemal's statement's at the time of the Hildebrand interview because Mustafa Kemal decided there would be no news at all whilst the Independence Tribunal prepared indictments and arrest warrants. The *Hakimiyet-i-Milliye* was not printed between the 22nd June and the 25th

---

1 Kinross, p. 427.
2 Mango, p. 445.
3 Ibid., p. 446.
4 Erik Jan Zürcher, *The Unionist Factor: The Role of the Committee of Union and Progress in the Turkish National Movement, 1905-1926* (Leiden: E. J. Brill, 1984), p. 148.
5 Mango, p. 449.
6 Ataöv, p. 63.

June, 1926.[1] When the Turkish Government was ready to share news, publication recommenced on the 26th, the same day the Independence Tribunal, with an agreed narrative, began the first trials.[2]

At this point it is worth considering again, the issue of domestic and international audiences. Mustafa Kemal had proven himself a brilliant military tactical strategist, skills he was able to utilise in his pursuit of political and diplomatic objectives. Mustafa Kemal was surely shrewd enough to understand the necessity of shaping different messages to different audiences. With this in mind, why would Mustafa Kemal want such an interview published in Turkey? The message in the Hildebrand interview was surely intended for a foreign audience. Publishing the interview in Turkey would have been damaging for two reasons. Firstly, it would have pre-empted the Court's decisions, suggesting that Mustafa Kemal had already decided the guilt or innocence of the conspirators. Secondly, and more damagingly, the Hildebrand interview would not have played well with those elements of Turkish society that still had high regard for the cadre of military leaders who now stood accused. William Hale in his authoritative work on the history and role of the Turkish military records, "The arrest of Ali Fuat [Cebesoy] and the other generals caused quite a stir. During the trials they were saluted by their brother officers and hailed by the public wherever they went."[3] Hale goes on to say, if Mustafa Kemal's plan had been to pillory them, it backfired and he quickly intervened to order their release during the trials. It is a reasonable assumption therefore to conclude that the Hildebrand Interview and the views expressed were never intended for a domestic hearing.[4]

1 Ibid.
2 Mango, p. 448.
3 William Hale, *Turkish Politics and the Military* (Routledge, 2013), p. 75.
4 This is a point made by Erik Zürcher, who whilst acknowledging the doubts raised by Ataöv concludes the alleged Hildebrand Interview was aimed an international audience. See Erik J Zürcher, *The Young Turk Legacy and Nation Building: From the Ottoman Empire to Atatürk's Turkey*, vol. 87 (IB Tauris, 2014).

The Style and Wording in the Hildebrand Interview – "Totally Alien Rhetoric" or Plausible?

Ataöv contends that Mustafa Kemal's recorded courteousness meant he was incapable of "the wild and heedless phraseology attributed to him, the interview style was "totally alien rhetoric."[1] He asserts that Mustafa Kemal "possessed a distinctive elegance in speech and writing," and furthermore, "had an overall manner and smartness peculiar to himself so evident in all his conversations, oral communications and written words." In Ataöv's view therefore, the intemperate words attributed to Mustafa Kemal in the Hildebrand interview prove its inauthenticity.

Although Mustafa Kemal's general demeanour can certainly be characterised as courteous, examples do exist that illustrate he was capable of human anger, intemperate language and threats. Alexander Lyon Macfie refers to Mustafa Kemal's "irascible temper."[2] Macfie recounts an incident when Mustafa Kemal was aroused to "feelings of great anger" over the attempt of the Sultan's Government to defeat the national movement during the Sivas Congress in 1919. "On the 10th September, happening to be present in the telegraph office during an exchange of telegrams he dashed off," an angry missive to Adil Bey, Minister of the Interior. Mustafa Kemal calls the Turkish Government, "cowards and criminals," and cannot believe, "you can play the part of traitors to and executioners of the nation." Even more telling is the implicit threat, "You had better think well what you are doing. Beware lest the day should come when you will be called upon to render account to the nation...."[3] Mango quotes from the *Nutuk* which refers to fellow Turks as "Wretches, murders, traitors. You are plotting with the enemy against the State."[4]

1 Ataöv, p. 59.
2 Alexander Lyon Macfie, *Ataturk* (Routledge, 2014), p. 46.
3 Ibid., pp. 77-78.
4 Mango, pp. 250-51.

Another incident where Mustafa Kemal's temper frayed is recorded by Şukran Vahide in his biography of Kurdish Muslim Theologian Bediüzzaman Said Nursî. Vahide cites an outburst by Mustafa Kemal directed at Said Nursî in the assembly. Other Assembly members feared for Nursî, but Mustafa Kemal, aware of Nursî's influence with traditionalists, "suppressed his anger and in effect apologised two days later."[1]

There are other instances of intemperate behaviour. Alexander Macfie cites the memoirs of Halide Edib, the notable and exceptional Turkish feminist and Independence War heroine. "In the course of the battle [of Sakarya] Mustafa Kemal remained for the most part, at the headquarters at Alagöz where Halide Edib observed him fuming, swearing, walking up and down, talking loudly..."[2] On another occasion Mustafa Kemal "flew into a violent rage," over the sentiments expressed in a British newspaper report on Turkey.[3] Halide Edib also recalls Mustafa Kemal's,

> ...open quarrel with Hamdullah Soubhi Bey. In a heated discussion, he called Hamdullah Soubhi Bey a liar, and he in turn demanded that Mustafa Kemal Pasha should take his word back. This he did, but at the same time he began his usual clever underhand propaganda against Hamdullah Soubhi Bey.[4]

In the *Nutuk*, Mustafa Kemal's long speech outlining the history of the Turkish nation, he "belittled" the role of his opponents in the independence struggle. Zürcher writes, "at least 52 passages are

1 Sukran Vahide, *Islam in Modern Turkey: An Intellectual Biography of Bediuzzaman Said Nursi* (Suny Press, 2012), p. 171.
2 Macfie, p. 123.
3 George Gawrych, *The Young Atatürk: From Ottoman Soldier to Statesman of Turkey* (IB Tauris, 2013), p. 126.
4 Halide Edib Adıvar, *The Turkish Ordeal: Being the Further Memoirs of Halidé Edib* (New York, London: The Century Company 1928).

devoted to criticism, innuendo and sarcasm directed against the former opposition leaders."[1]

Of greater significance are the circumstances pertaining to an interview of Mustafa Kemal by a foreign correspondent that is interesting on two counts. The original interview contained fiery language and resulted a heavily edited and censored account.[2] Hakan Özoğlu explores Mustafa Kemal's attitude to the announcement of the formation of the opposition Progressive Republican Party (PRP). Whilst there are records of Mustafa Kemal welcoming the idea of an opposition party from the memoirs of his inner circle, Hakan Özoğlu quotes from an archival consular source that provides an entirely different perspective. On the 25th November 1924, British Ambassador to Turkey, Sir Rodney Lindsay sent a consular report to London containing a transcript of a newspaper interview with Mustafa Kemal. The interview had been conducted a few days earlier by the *Times* Turkey Correspondent, a seasoned WWI journalist named Maxwell Macartney. Lindsay attached his own postscript based on Macartney's account of the meeting and the mood of Mustafa Kemal.[3] Sir Rodney's report begins with a reference to Mustafa Kemal's stance to the establishment of the opposition PRP and is described as "a war to the knife."

> If I have been wondering what the President will do next, here is an answer for me in this very remarkable document [the text of the Macartney Interview 21st November 1924]. The Progressives [the PRP] are insincere in their republicanism, their programme is a fraud, and they are mere reactionaries. Everything reported implies the President will have nothing to do with the new opposition, and his language to Mr Macartney, not reported, and the tone of the

---

1 Zürcher, *The Young Turk Legacy and Nation Building: From the Ottoman Empire to Atatürk's Turkey*, 87, p. 13.
2 Mango, p. 420.
3 Hakan Özoğlu, *From Caliphate to Secular State: Power Struggle in the Early Turkish Republic* (ABC-CLIO, 2011), pp. 87-88.

remarks indicated clearly that he meant war to the knife. The Ghazi worked himself up into a perfect frenzy; he turned red in the face as he ticked off each member of the opposition in turn, characterising them as ungrateful to himself, to whom they owed all, and traitors to their country. The deputy who acted at the interview as introducer and half as interpreter interrupted more than once, exclaiming: Be calm "Ghazi Pasha, do not be so indiscreet," but nothing could check the flood of indignation. Mr. Macartney has come away from Angora thinking that pistols will be going off in earnest in a very short time, and that Massif and Nejati have left the government in order to come down to Constantinople at the head of a more business like Tribunal of Independence which will decorate the Galata Bridge with hanging of corpses.[1]

The phraseology attributed to Mustafa Kemal in the Macartney interview is similar in tone to that reported in the Hildebrand article that includes phrases such as, "I shall not stop until [all] have been hung from gallows."

Lest those of a conspiratorial mind-set question the suppression of the report in the *Times*, by suggesting its non-inclusion somehow casts doubt on the diplomatic account, it is worth examining the circumstances. The reason why Macartney judged it prudent to self-censor his own article is not difficult to establish. The clue is contained in his advice to colleagues a few years later. Maxwell H. H. Macartney, the *Times* correspondent was a seasoned journalist who understood antagonising powerful political heads of state would result in expulsion. As the *Times* correspondent in fascist Italy, Macartney issued some humorous advice to other correspondents. A colleague from the United Press filed a report stating Mussolini had been taken ill and was immediately expelled from Italy. According to Maxwell

---

1 Erik Jan Zürcher, *Political Opposition in the Early Turkish Republic: The Progressive Republican Party, 1924-1925*, vol. 44 (Leiden; New York: EJ Brill, 1991) and Özoğlu, pp. 87-88.

Macartney, the "three sacrosanct rules" for reporters[1] in authoritarian Italy were:

> You never write anything that hints the lira isn't sound. You never write anything that casts doubts on the valour of the Italian army. And you certainly, at no time, do you dare hint that the Duce is not a [Rock of] Gibraltar of good health.[2]

Similar sensitivities existed in Turkey which would also lead to an abrupt expulsion for journalists transgressing the unwritten rules. Indeed, this did occur a few years after Macartney's 1924 self-censored report in April 1926, when the *Times* correspondent to Turkey was expelled for a story of minor importance that nevertheless upset the Turkish authorities. Not only does this article explain the circumstances of the expulsion, but reveals that by April 1926, the Turkish authorities had started to censor and halt telegrams sent by foreign correspondents of which it disapproved.[3] Macartney's self-censorship of Mustafa Kemal's intemperate words served to ensure he could remain in position in 1924.

Finally, there remains the question as to how might Hildebrand have established contact with the Worldwide News Services and provided it with his copy. Nearly a hundred years have passed so it is unlikely that question can be answered. However, it is possible to establish that Hildebrand had a working relationship with a Swedish-American journalist by the name of Axel Fredenholm. Again it is impossible to establish precise timelines but Fredenholm appears to have been living in the United States and had been an active member of the US based Swedish American Historical Society.[4] Fredenholm is

---

1 John Patrick Diggins, *Mussolini and Fascism: The View from America* (Princeton University Press, 2015), p. 318.
2 Ibid., p. 318.
3 See the article of the *Times* 3 April 1926. 'The Turks & "the Times" - Our Correspondent's Expulsion - A Suppressed Message' The correspondent
4 Fredenholm, Axel. Year Book of the Swedish-American Historical Society 1916-17 Sångoffer Till Severige. pp. 88. http://runeberg.org/ybswedam/6/0011.html. Accessed 10/2/2018.

also listed as the editor of *Österns Veckoblada*, a Swedish language newspaper, on a list of editors issuing an appeal for the US not to go to war in 1915.[1] According to US Library of Congress records the newspaper was published from the city of Worcester between 1907 and 1924[2]. In 1924 and 1925 Hildebrand and Fredenholm co-edited a book on Swedish migrants in the US that was published in 1926.[3] If Hildebrand required a conduit into the US, is it not reasonable to hypothesise he might have turned to a current co-author who had served as a journalist and editor in the US? And for those not familiar with US geography, Worcester is a city in the state of Massachusetts less than fifty miles from Boston and the home of the Worldwide News Service in 1926.

Enver Paşa: Utmost Respect or a "Fool-Sycophant"?

The relationship between Mustafa Kemal and his rival Enver Paşa, the Young Turk leader and his former superior is discussed by Ataöv. Despite the two men's intense rivalry, Ataöv states Mustafa Kemal "was never heard making a humiliating remark about Enver Paşa." This, Ataöv asserts, is "in spite of disagreements on policy, dissimilarities in character and understandable competition between the two..."[4] To

---

1 See "An Appeal to the American People," published in various newspapers including *The News Journal* (Wilmington, Delaware) and the *Washington Times*. All published 5th April 1915, p. 8 & 7 respectively. Fredenholm is included in the long list of editors and their respective newspapers.

2 See the Library of Congress Records on historic US newspapers. https://chroniclingamerica.loc.gov/lccn/sn00062065/ Accessed 10/2/2018

3 See Barton, Hildor Arnold. *A Folk Divided: Homeland Swedes and Swedish Americans, 1840-1940*, Vol. 10, SIU Press, 1994. pp 277. Hildebrand, Karl Emil Hildebrand, and Axel Fredenholm. Svenskarna i Amerika. Populär historisk skildring i ord och bild av svenskarnas liv och underbara öden i Förenta Staterna och Canada. Historiska Förlaget, 1926. ISBN B004RCTHF6

4 Ataöv, p. 60.

say that Mustafa Kemal never said a bad word about Enver is contradicted by various sources.

The antagonism between Mustafa Kemal and Enver Paşa long predated WWI and is laid-out in some detail by Zürcher.[1] Kinross refers to the level of enmity between the CUP leadership and Mustafa Kemal. Having disagreed with the CUP leadership and been outvoted on the Army's role in politics, Mustafa Kemal was marked down for liquidation. The first attempt failed and when a second attempt was undertaken by the uncle of Enver, this also failed as the result of a tip-off.[2]

The enmity continued during WWI. Dadrian refers to the memoirs of the valet to Heinz Foelner, the German Chief Engineer of the Baghdad Railway, and states that Foelner paid host to Mustafa Kemal's visit to Aleppo in the autumn of 1918. In an account of these meetings in his memoirs, the valet quotes Mustafa Kemal's repeated denunciation of both Enver and Talaat in strong language. Enver was described by Mustafa Kemal as a '*ahmak-yaltak*' (fool-sycophant) and Talaat, a "gypsy son of a bitch." He regarded Enver and Talaat as, "… the kind of men who should be hanged, great assassins"[3] It is possible the valet, who appears to have been Armenian, might have had an axe to grind against the Young Turks, but not, it would seem, against Mustafa Kemal. In fact another more authoritative record backs up the valet's account of Mustafa Kemal contemptuous attitude to Enver. After the catastrophic defeat of the Turkish 8th Army's at the Battle of Megiddo (September 1918), Mustafa Kemal's 7th Army was left to face the advancing British forces. He succeeded in keeping his own forces largely intact, but was infuriated by the decimation of the entire 8th Army. In a telegram to the Sultan, he was forthright in his view of Enver Paşa. The 8th Army withdrawal "could have been carried out in

1 Erik Jan Zürcher, "Atatürk as a Young Turk," *New Perspectives on Turkey* 41 (2009): pp. 211-26.
2 Kinross, p. 39.
3 Dadrian, p. 131.

some order, if a fool like Enver Paşa had not been the director-general of the operations..."[1]

In the years preceding and during the infancy of the new Turkish Republic, Mustafa Kemal might well have refrained from making further derogatory remark about Enver. The simple truth was that Mustafa Kemal's position and that of his Nationalist supporters was precarious. The exiled Enver had allied himself with the Russian Bolsheviks and maintained links to anti-Kemalist groupings in Turkey.[2] The machinations of Enver's Unionist allies, still active in Turkey, constituted an existential threat to the new Kemalist Republic.[3] Enver and his wartime accomplice, Talaat, remained an active threat. As Şuhnaz Yilmaz says, "Enver's intentions, in particular, were far removed from the idea of withdrawing to a quiet corner, leaving the political and the military arena. He viewed the situation only as a temporary setback: a tactical retreat to resume fighting after gathering some strength."[4]

There is documentary evidence of the exiled Enver's attempt to curry favour with Mustafa Kemal contained in correspondence between the two men. Enver attempted to assure Mustafa Kemal of his loyalty to the nationalist cause and his contentment with playing a role outside of Turkey by promoting pan-Turkism under the aegis of Islam and with the support of the Bolshevik state. Enver wrote,

> If you consider us [the Unionists] as a rival, you are making a big mistake. We are not after any titles or positions. As far as I am concerned, I will follow my ideals. That is to incite the Muslims to struggle against the European beasts which trample upon Islam. By the news

---

1 Mango, p. 179.
2 Edmund Burke III, *Subversives and Mavericks in the Muslim Mediterranean: A Subaltern History* (University of Texas Press, 2016), pp. 152-53.
3 Şuhnaz Yilmaz, "An Ottoman Warrior Abroad: Enver Paşa as an Expatriate," *Middle Eastern Studies* 35, no. 4 (1999): pp. 40-69.
4 Ibid., p. 48.

which you have been sending through my friends, I understand that you do not want us to return. For the time being, since we are being helpful to our motherland in Moscow, we are not coming back. However, when we start to feel that... our staying abroad becomes useless and even dangerous for Turkey and the Islamic world, we will return to Anatolia.[1]

Mustafa Kemal and the other Kemalists distrusted these assurances and with good reason. The Kemalists intercepted a Unionist agent, Major Nairn Cevad, whom Enver had sent from Russia to Turkey. He was found to be in possession of large quantities of propaganda material for use by the dormant network of Enver supporters. Whilst Enver talked of national solidarity and in December 1921 dreamed of leading a so-called pan-Turkish, Muslim Green Army (*Yeşil Ordu*) to fight Greek invaders, there was no doubt their objective was the elimination of the Kemalists too. Talaat Pasha, Enver's triumvirate partner was explicit in a letter to Enver's cousin written in 1921, that "...there should be no mercy towards these men (Kemalists) anymore. We must be prepared for a full-scale revolution, a bloody revolution."[2]

This subject has been covered in exhaustive detail by Salahi Sonyel utilising a variety of sources including Turkish telegrams and declassified British Intelligence reports from their headquarters in Istanbul.[3] Enver and his acolytes were prevented from returning to Turkey and orders were issued for their arrest should they do so.[4]

By the summer of 1921, the Kemalists feared Enver was about to launch a coup d'état against Mustafa Kemal. The *Hakimiyet-i-Milliye* the semi-official Kemalist newspaper that had been founded by and whose editor, Ahmet Ağaoğlu had been appointed by Mustafa Kemal a

1 Letter from Enver Pasha to Mustafa Kemal dated 4 Oct. 1920, in Ali Fuat Cebesoy, *Moskova Hatiralari,* (Istanbul, 1955), p. 231.
2 Yilmaz, pp. 52-53.
3 Salahi R. Sonyel, "Mustafa Kemal and Enver in Conflict, 1919–22," ibid. 25 (1989): pp. 506-15.
4 Macfie, p. 107.

year earlier, went on the offensive.[1] The newspaper attacked the record and ambitions of the old CUP and the unionists, accusing them of having destroyed the Ottoman Empire and wishing the same for Turkey.[2] Foreign newspapers too, reported the remarks of Kemalist leaders criticising Enver's ambitions. The *Times* reported a speech by Mustafa Kemal himself to the Ankara Assembly in which he castigated those "…deceivers of the masses or chasers of mirages."[3]

In short, the suggestion that the Hildebrand interview is inauthentic because it contains derogatory remarks by Mustafa Kemal about Enver Paşa is not plausible. Rather, it is more likely to be authentic *because* the views expressed are exactly in line with Mustafa Kemal's previously documented opinions.

The Izmir Conspiracy

The assassination plot as described by Ataöv is a circumscribed and simplified description of events. In Ataöv's account the essential elements were these: on the 7th May 1926 Mustafa Kemal left Ankara to embark on a nation-wide tour. He arrived in Bursa at the beginning of June intending to travel onto Izmir, but received a telegram from the city's governor informing him a plot had been discovered. He delayed his journey and waited as details of the plot emerged. A boatman named Şevki (of Crete) had informed the police of his role to assassinate Mustafa Kemal in Izmir on 15th June 1926, the very next day. Şevki's role was to spirit away the assassins by boat to neighbouring islands. Şevki named Ziya Hurşit, "a reckless ex-deputy" of the previous assembly as the organiser. That same night, Ziya Hurşit was arrested in his Izmir hotel room where bombs and guns were found. During interrogation, Ziya Hurşit confessed and led the

---

1 For a detailed background on Ahmet Agaoglu see: A Holly Shissler, *Between Two Empires: Ahmet Agaoglu and the New Turkey* (IB Tauris, 2002).
2 Sonyel, p. 512.
3 Special Correspondent, 'New Dangers for Angora - Hopes of Moderation,' Despatch dated 12 Dec. Printed The Times, 15 December 1921, London.

police to "other collaborators, some of whom were notorious as adventurous gunmen."[1]

Ataöv points to the contradiction between this version of events and those described in the Hildebrand article; the informant was a boatman originating from Crete whereas the article referred to a lady. He asserts, "this error alone is sufficient to prove that the whole statement attributed to Mustafa Kemal is a forgery."[2] Was this an error and if so, why would the so-called fabricator make such an obvious mistake? Is it possible a woman, rather than Giritli Şevki the Cretan boatman was involved in tipping off the authorities about an intended assassination on June 15th 1926? The Hildebrand interview has Mustafa Kemal stating the following:

> They went even further and seduced a woman who had been for years identified with my cause and who had been my loyal political friend and on occasion, even adviser. They induced this woman to accept the reprehensible assignment to present me with a bouquet which concealed a bomb that would, on my receiving it, explode and obliterate everyone in sight. This ill-advised woman deserves pity, for she was made to believe that she would thus sacrifice her own life for the good of the fatherland. I was the enemy of the nation. She will be forgiven for her part in the plot, for she conscience-stricken, confessed to the proper authorities in time for me to cancel my intended tour.

In his account of the attempted Izmir assassination, Ataöv makes a key mistake in his recounting of Mustafa Kemal's movements. His form of words suggest that Mustafa Kemal's delay was caused by his receiving "a most urgent telegram" informing him a plot had been discovered *after* Şevki the boatman confessed.[3] This is incorrect and misleading. An examination of the timetable of events gives credence that someone informed the authorities of an intended assassination

---

1 Ataöv, pp. 57-58.
2 Ibid.
3 Ibid., p. 57.

before Şevki the boatman confessed. According to the published Presidential Tour, Mustafa Kemal was to leave Bursa on the 14th June 1926 and travel by train to arrive in Izmir on the morning of 15th June where a mansion in nearby Çeşme had been prepared for his stay in the area. However, on the 14th June, after travelling less than half the distance to Izmir, Mustafa Kemal halted the presidential train at Balıkesir some 180 kilometres north of Izmir. The next morning's schedule tour of Izmir was cancelled and Mustafa Kemal remained at Balıkesir overnight and for the duration of 15th June.[1]

The effect of Mustafa Kemal's non-arrival at Izmir on the 15th June had an almost immediate consequence; Şevki, the Cretan boatman panicked and fearing the plot was discovered, is reported to have handed himself in to the authorities. In other words, Mustafa Kemal did not abort his Izmir 15th June schedule *because* of Giritli Şevki's confession, he had already halted his journey. The timing of Şevki's confession to a police inspector came late in the evening of the 15th June, "towards 11'oclock."[2] The governor of Izmir, General Kâzım Dirik a former staff officer to Mustafa Kemal, "swung into action." Ziya Hurşit and the other conspirators on the scene were arrested in their hotel rooms that same evening.[3] A telegram *was then* sent to Mustafa Kemal detailing the circumstances of the plot to kill him scheduled to have occurred earlier that day.[4] With the assassins in custody, Mustafa Kemal remained in Balıkesir before continuing his journey to Izmir on the morning of 16th June where he addressed enthusiastic crowds on his arrival later that day.[5]

At issue is why Mustafa Kemal's train came to a halt on the 14th June,180 kilometres from his destination and proceeded no further *before* Şevki's confession to the authorities in Izmir? For Kinross, Mustafa Kemal's decision not to proceed suggests a sixth sense.

---

1 Mango, p. 445.
2 Ibid., p. 445.
3 Kinross, p. 427.
4 Özoğlu, p. 125.
5 Kinross, p. 427.

He had delayed his arrival from Balıkesir and thus perhaps
saved his life for no other reason than an instinct which may
have been a presentiment.[1]

Although the notion of Mustafa Kemal possessing a mystical sixth-
sense is attractive to those of a haliographic mind-set, it is an
unconvincing as a rational explanation. The more likely explanation is
the one contained in the Hildebrand interview; Mustafa Kemal was in
receipt of information of a possible plot – a possibility entertained by
Macfie.[2] The delay at Balıkesir allowed the authorities to make further
investigations and this appears to have facilitated Giritli Şevki's
decision to confess. In this light, Ataöv's conclusion that the
suggestion of another informant in the Hildebrand interview proves it
a forgery, is countered.[3] What no one to date can explain is how did
Mustafa Kemal know to stop his train on 14th June, *before* Giritli
Şevki's confession? The Hildebrand interview arguably provides a
missing piece of the jigsaw by providing an explanation for the delay
at Balıkesir: Mustafa Kemal received urgent news from a woman with
knowledge of an imminent attempt on his life at Izmir.

If this is true, who could this woman informant be? A person "who
had been for years identified with my cause and who had been my
loyal political friend and on occasion, even adviser." There can only be
a few possible candidates given the restrictive and subservient role
women had endured under Ottoman rule. The experience of war and
the demands for labour had facilitated new thinking and new
opportunities and a handful of women had challenged cultural
stereotypes and achieved some national recognition as intellectuals
and/or leaders in their field.[4] Whilst one can identify individuals such
as Nezihe Muhiddin (1889-1958) and Nakiye Elgün as active in the
correct timescale, they cannot be described as close to Mustafa

---

1 Ibid.
2 Macfie.
3 Ataöv, p. 58.
4 Emine Nermin Abadan-Unat and Deniz Kandiyoti, *Women in Turkish
Society*, vol. 30 (Brill, 1981), pp. 8-10.

Kemal.[1] Moreover, the 1926 plot had no bearing on their subsequent careers and they continued to live in Turkey. The most likely candidate is Halide Edib Adıvar, who had served as a confidante and advisor in the period up to and after the War of Independence.[2] She worked "as a writer and translator of [Mustafa Kemal] Atatürk, accompanying him on military expeditions to the front lines and at times taking part in the fighting. Mustafa Kemal promoted her from corporal to major."[3] She was married to Dr. Adnan Adıvar, a Minister of Health and Minister of the Interior in Mustafa Kemal's pre-Republic 1920 Government and then a Deputy Speaker (Vice President) of the Turkish Parliament.[4]

There is no doubt that both Adnan Adıvar and his wife Halide Edib harboured growing concerns with the direction in which Mustafa Kemal was taking the country. They had belonged to the less radical wing of Mustafa Kemal's People's Party (PP) that favoured a more transitional approach to a liberal democracy, possibly within a monarchist framework.[5] Halide Edib was more 'conservative' in that she had always envisaged a future Turkey rooted in its Islamic past; modern and liberal, but not necessarily secular, a view recounted in her early autobiography.[6] She had previously argued that Islamic Law

---

1 Katharina Knaus, "Turkish Women: A Century of Change," *Turkish Policy Quarterly* 6, no. 5 (2007): p. 53-56. Ayça Ülker Erkan, "The Formation of Feminist Identity: Feminism in the 1930's Turkey and Britain," (Eylül, 2011), p. 1021.
2 Francisca de Haan, Krassimira Daskalova, and Anna Loutfi, *Biographical Dictionary of Women's Movements and Feminisms in Central, Eastern, and South Eastern Europe: 19th and 20th Centuries* (Central European University Press, 2006), p. 122.
3 Helen Rappaport, *Encyclopedia of Women Social Reformers*, vol. 1 (Abc-clio, 2001), p. 218.
4 Clifford Edmund Bosworth, *The Encyclopaedia of Islam, New Edition: Supplement* (Brill Archive, 1980), p. 41.
5 Selim Deringil, "Political Opposition in the Early Turkish Republic: The Progressive Republican Party 1924-1925," (JSTOR, 1994), p. 157.
6 Halide Edib, *The Turkish Ordeal. Being the Further Memoirs of Halide Edib* (Century Company, 1928).

was in many respects more favourable to women than western law.[1] The announcement of a Turkish Republic in October 1923 with Mustafa Kemal as its new President occurred whilst the Adıvars and other leading politicians were still in Istanbul and absent from the newly announced capital, Ankara. As the new President, Mustafa Kemal appointed a new Prime Minister without consulting the Adıvars and their colleagues, both Adıvar and the other Independence War leaders reacted angrily to the proclamation in the Istanbul press, calling the decision premature and stressing that calling the state a republic did not in itself bring freedom and the real difference was between despotism and democracy.[2]

Eric Zürcher devotes a chapter of his book, *Turkey: A Modern History*, to the rising tensions in the aftermath of the proclaimed republic, outlining how this element of PRP members increasingly felt the country was being led towards dictatorship and their own positions might have been in danger.[3] One example was the experience of former Prime Minister Rauf Orbay, who, having criticised the decision to declare a republic to the press, was summoned to a meeting of the PP where his loyalty to the new regime was questioned.[4] These transitionalist-minded members of the PP must have been aware they were treading a fine line in their opposition to the Kemalists. The 1920 *Hiyanet-i Vatanaye* (High Treason Law) which had been amended in March 1923 made it illegal to support the restoration of the Turkish monarchy.[5] At some point in 1924 the transitionalists began to discuss breaking from the monolithic PP and forming their own party. The Progressive Republican People's Party (PRP) came into official existence in November 1924 with Dr. Adnan

1 de Haan, Daskalova, and Loutfi, p. 121; Halide Edib, *Conflict of East and West in Turkey*, (1935), p. 53.
2 Zürcher, *Turkey: A Modern History*, Chap 10.
3 Ibid.
4 Özoğlu, p. 86.
5 Carter V. Findley, *Turkey, Islam, Nationalism, and Modernity: A History, 1789-2007* (Yale University Press, 2010), Chap 5.

Halide Edib and Mustafa Kemal, Ankara.

Adıvar as its General Secretary. The new Party leader was General Kâzım Karabekir. According to Rauf Orbay the PRP's prime objective was the "preventing of a personal dictatorship…"[1]

The decision to engage in political opposition to Mustafa Kemal appears to have led Adnan Adıvar and Halide Edib to make arrangements to secure their own safety by establishing a 'safe house' in England in early 1924.[2] They appear to have moved back and forwards between their home in England and Turkey giving rise to a general confusion as to when the husband and wife pair went into permanent exile.

A careful trawl of newspaper archives confirms that the pair established a second home in England in 1924 but remained active in Turkish politics.[3] In November 1925, an article appeared in the *Manchester Guardian* featuring an interview with Halide Edib that confirms she and her husband were renting a bungalow in the English Chiltern Hills. She is described as "the leader of the women's movement in Turkey."[4] Evidence of Halide Edib's on-going activity in Turkish politics whilst flitting between different countries can be gleaned from other sources to show that she was still active in Turkish politics. She is described as working with the Turkish Union of Women and announcing her decision in 1925 to stand for election in order to force the issue of female suffrage.[5] This is confirmed by a *New York Times* piece, attributed to the Constantinople correspondent of the *Chicago Tribune,* recording her as having been nominated for

---

1 Özoğlu, p. 85.

2 Correspondent, "Politics Institute Calls a Feminist," *New York Times,* 28th May 1928.

3 In addition to the previous source stating 1924, another article in the *New York Times,* 28th May 1928 records 1924 as the year, "she and her husband went to England, where they have been living since then."

4 Sharp, Evelyn. "A Turkish Woman Leader - The Young Turk and Women's Freedom," *Manchester Guardian,* 4th November 1925.

5 Chicago Tribune Co. Copyright Syndicate, "Turkish Women Nominated," *The New York Times,* 2nd March 1925.

office in February 1925.[1] The significance of these reports lies in the fact that despite living in England in 1924 onwards, they both remained a key part of Turkish opposition politics.

The *Manchester Guardian* is important in another respect too; it provides an insight into her attitude towards the Kemalists and the motivation for her move towards the PRP. Her sympathies towards the old CUP are laid bare. Their positive attitude towards women, she asserts, was almost "the best thing about the Young Turk movement." The article refers to her attitude to the new Turkish Government's policies on the fez and veil in critical terms. These are characterised as "silly and not inspired by women." Rather it was the Kemalists, these changes in Turkish society "...were being imposed by a narrow clique," and the new laws formed "part of the westernising policy of the present Government, and is approved mainly by the high officials and the 'new rich'..." And should the reader be in any doubt of her views on the Turkish Government, she describes it as a "dictatorship."[2]

In the period from 1924 up to the end of January 1926, Halide Edib's husband Adnan Adıvar also continued his political activities, sitting in the Assembly as a PRP opposition member (and as an independent after the PRP's abolition).[3] Perhaps more significantly, he was at the very centre of the new Party's activities given his position as General Secretary. In that role, he attended a meeting with Mustafa Kemal's Prime Minister, along with PRP leader Karabekir to discuss and resist a Government request to voluntarily close down the Party.[4] After the forced closure of the PRP structure in June 1925, Adıvar

---

1 See "Turkish Women Nominated", *New York Times*, 2nd March 1928.

2 Evelyn Sharp, "A Turkish Woman Leader - The Young Turk and Women's Freedom," *The Manchester Guardian*, 4th November 1925.

3 Stanford J. Shaw and Ezel Kural Shaw, *History of the Ottoman Empire and Modern Turkey: Volume 2, Reform, Revolution, and Republic: The Rise of Modern Turkey 1808-1975*, vol. 11 (Cambridge University Press, 1977), p. 468.

4 Zürcher, *Political Opposition in the Early Turkish Republic: The Progressive Republican Party, 1924-1925*, 44, p. 82.

remained as a sitting PRP member of the Assembly until tendering his resignation at the end of January 1926 and removing himself back to England where he stayed whilst the plot unfolded.[1]

What prompted Adıvar's resignation and the decision to absent himself from Turkey? Was it the wish to avoid association with an impending distasteful deed and the need to provide an alibi? This was certainly the view of Mustafa Kemal following the foiled assassination attempt. Mustafa Kemal telegrammed his Prime Minister, Ismet Pasha, on the 18th June 1926:

> The decision for the assassination was made collectively by all the members of [the PRP's] general committee… it is telling that Rauf Bey left earlier for Europe, Kazim Karabekir met secretly with Ziya Hurst in Ankara,… and Adnan Bey [Adıvar] extended his stay in London… Therefore, it is necessary to arrest and punish all leaders and some members of the PRP.[2]

There is also some evidence that Adnan Adıvar and his wife Halide Edib thought the new Party they had helped found, the PRP, was over-stepping the mark in its opposition to Mustafa Kemal. Eric Zürcher quotes a diplomatic report in which the pair are recorded as saying, "things went too far."[3] The role of Adnan Adıvar and in particular his wife Halide Edib are examined in more detail later.

There is a counter argument Mustafa Kemal merely used the Izmir incident to justify a general crackdown and the arrest of the remnants

---

1 Office of the Prime Minister, "Health Personnel Serving in the First Term of the Turkish National Assembly," Ataturk Cultural Center, http://www.atam.gov.tr/dergi/sayi-42/turkiye-millet-meclisi-birinci-doneminde-gorev-yapan-saglik-mensuplari. Accessed 12/2/2017. Feza Günergun, "Adnan Adıvar's Works in History of Science: Prior to the 'La Science Chez Les Turcs Ottomans' and Thereafter," *Osmanlı Bilimi Araştırmaları (Studies in Ottoman Science)* 7, no. 2 - 1 (2006): p. 1.
2 Özoğlu, p. 128.
3 Zürcher, *Political Opposition in the Early Turkish Republic: The Progressive Republican Party, 1924-1925*, 44, p. 107.

of the PRP. For example, William Hale writes, Mustafa Kemal, "evidently decided to widen the circle of accused so as to eliminate all his actual potential rivals at a stroke."[1] However Hale offers nothing in the way to support this interpretation. Haken Özoğlu suggests the proof that Mustafa Kemal exploited the situation to order the arrest of PRP leaders is the simple fact that the conspirator Ziya Hurşit explicitly refused to implicate them. However, the sentiments in the Hildebrand reveal an entirely different explanation. The female informant who had confessed directly to Mustafa Kemal revealed a far wider conspiracy. This conspiracy was a variant of "will no one rid me of this turbulent priest?" with Mustafa Kemal cast as the troublesome dictator. Except of course, in this variation, Mustafa Kemal's former colleagues knew what foul deed was afoot if not the precise details. In this context Mustafa's reaction and clampdown was not just a cynical manoeuvre to suppress all opposition. It is possible Mustafa Kemal was both shocked and alarmed by the treachery of those he considered old comrades and their complicity in a plot to murder him to change the Republic's development. As Özoğlu acknowledges, "Mustafa Kemal seems to be genuinely suspicious of the counter revolutionary potential of the assassination plot."[2]

There is evidence of PRP involvement in plotting to remove or kill Mustafa Kemal. The varied nature of possible assassination plots considered by Ziya Hurşit is recounted by Kinross and establishes that the Izmir June 15th plot was merely the outcome of aborted schemes planned for Ankara. One plan involved Ziya Hurşit reconnoitring the parliament building to ascertain the practicality of lobbing a bomb from the stranger's gallery into the presidential box. Another plan involved him forcing a hole in the roof of the parliament from which to shoot Mustafa Kemal. Yet another plan to rush a cabinet meeting was dismissed because of tight security.[3]

---

1 Hale, p. 75.
2 Özoğlu, p. 128.
3 Kinross, pp. 425-26.

Press reports of the time state the Independence Tribunal itself alleged the decision to kill Mustafa Kemal had started in December 1925 by a "band of individuals" associated with the opposition.[1] Mango believes the plotting started with the return of Ziya Hurşit from Istanbul to Ankara at the end of 1925. Ziya Hurşit began visiting the former members of the PRP. It is not known for certain which ex PRP members Ziya Hurşit visited, but it included Assembly Member Ahmet Sükrü, Mehmet Arif Bey and his brother Faik Günday.[2] Of course, it is possible that the Turkish authorities exaggerated Ziya Hurşit's activities, but what is not in doubt is that he reconnoitred Ankara to assess the viability of various plots and met with members of the PRP in December 1925. Is it not plausible that Adıvar as a leading figure in the PRP (an Assembly Member and the Party's General Secretary) was aware of the plotting and the possibility it might come to fruition in the near future?[3] Is it possible that Halide Edib, not only knew of a plot, but had also been asked to participate and on second thoughts declined? Is this what explains the decision of the Adıvars to leave Turkey? This way they could play it safe and wait for the dirty deed to be done; out of reach from the Kemalists if the plotting went wrong and with an alibi, able to return if it succeeded.

Mustafa Kemal talks of a woman willing to sacrifice her life in the attempt to kill him. Was it plausible that Halide Edib would commit suicide for her beliefs? Psychologically she may well have fitted the profile of someone both willing to die for a cause and at the end of her tether physically and emotionally. On the one hand, she was a passionate idealist, committed to a vision. She had earned a strong reputation both as a patriotic orator and as a courageous soldier in the War of Independence.[4] But there were fragilities in her character too. Her autobiography contains references to mental disorders that

---

1 Staff Reporter, "Turkish Horror," *Sunday Times* (Perth), 18th July 1926.
2 Mango, pp. 443-44.
3 See http://en.writersofturkey.net/index.php?title=Halide_Edip_Ad%C4%B1var. Accessed 10/2/2018
4 Adıvar, pp. 135-36.

culminated in nervous breakdowns in her early years.[1] She appeared to entertain ideas of suicide, admitting at one point "to cease to be appeared to me as the highest felicity."[2] To add to her mental health woes, sometime in the mid-1920's Halide Edib began to suffer from chronic bowel and bladder problems for which she sought medical treatment in Carlsbad and Vienna.[3] Did her poor health and state of mind lead her to consider the ultimate sacrifice for her homeland?

There remains the question as to why Mustafa Kemal did not expose Halide Edib. It is impossible to say for certain; gratitude would be one such motive. In acting as she had, she had in all probability saved his life. In any case, to expose Halide Edib would have been damaging, as Mango says Mustafa Kemal "deserves his fame as the hero of women's emancipation..." and more importantly, Halide Edib was revered as the Turkish Joan of Arc.[4] Far better then to keep her out of the official narrative and allow her and her husband their lives on the condition they remained in exile. Another more practical reason in the early stages of the investigation might have been a perceived advantage in keeping what he knew from his enemies as he considered his moves. Indeed, this is precisely the modus operandi that Hakan Özoğlu suggests might have been at play regarding the earlier Sheikh Said Revolt and asks, "Did Mustafa Kemal have better intelligence than that of the government...[and] did not share it?"[5]

Ultimately, once the situation had been stabilised Mustafa Kemal would have appreciated there was a political advantage in drawing back the net. Whilst Halide Edib and her husband were spared in recognition of her act of loyalty, to unmask her would have shaken the foundations of the young Republic. With the bulk of the ex-Unionists

1 *House with Wisteria: Memoirs of Halidé Edib* (Leopolis Press, 2003), pp. 210 & 29.
2 Ibid., p. 192.
3 de Haan, Daskalova, and Loutfi, p. 122.
4 Mango, p. 438.
5 Özoğlu, p. 95.

captured and eliminated, it was not worth risking the people's support by executing a number of former war heroes. Mercy too may have played a part. Perhaps this was the 'deal' between Mustafa Kemal and Halide Edib; sparing her, her husband and the leadership of the PRP from the gallows in return for their contrition and exile.

For Halide Edib it must have been a bitter pill to swallow. Her betrayal of the plot saved Mustafa Kemal but had grave consequences. Whilst she might not have cared too much for the fate of opposition Unionist sympathisers such as Ziya Hurşit, she surely anguished over the impact on her PRP colleagues, not to mention her husband. As a group, they had experienced the gradual transition of the new Republic into a more authoritarian regime, seen newspapers closed, their Party disbanded and their reputations sullied. These experiences had fed their sense of grievance and an acceptance that bold measures must be taken to 'save' the nation from a perceived authoritarianism. When it came to it, despite her sense of personal grievance, she could not play Brutus to her Caesar. But nor could she hide in England, turning a blind eye to the looming assassination of a man she still admired and to who she recognised Turkey owed so much. In her second autobiography, penned in the aftermath of the assassination attempt, she concluded with a paragraph which served two purposes: a demonstration of her acceptance of the new Kemalist order and her exiled status, but also an explanation to her ex-PRP colleagues why she had acted to save Mustafa Kemal despite the wrongs she had felt.[1]

> All through the ordeal for independence the Turkish people itself has been the supreme hero—the Turkish people has honoured Mustafa Kemal Pasha as its symbol. For this reason, Mustafa Kemal Pasha will have a pedestal in the heart of every true Turk, even among those who have been irretrievably wronged by him.

1 Adıvar, *The Turkish Ordeal: Being the Further Memoirs of Halidé Edib*, Epilogue.

Conclusion

Professor Ataöv began his piece with a statement asserting, "it is actually the responsibility of the Armenian circles to prove the factuality and relevance of the so-called [Hildebrand] article…" This can only be partially correct; it is not the responsibility of Armenians to determine the truth, but rather the duty of all objective scholars.

It is not clear whether it is Ataöv's contention that Nercessian fabricated the *Los Angeles Examiner* interview or alternatively a group of Armenians invented the story in 1926. It is clearly not the former since the interview did without doubt appear in Hearst newspapers. Given that fact, what is Ataöv's asserting? It appears to be that in 1926 a group of émigré Armenians in Boston and Los Angeles conceived an elaborate plan involving a real journalist, a real news agency and a respected newspaper to print a fake story about the Turkish President. What would be the point if the Turkish Government (or the journalist or the News Agency) could simply deny it, and more to the point, what purpose would it serve in 1926 when most Americans accepted the fact of the Armenian massacres? Why for that matter would they wish to present Mustafa Kemal in a good light in the eyes of Americans? How too would these so called Armenian fabricators be party to information about the assassination before aspects of the circumstances had even been released in Turkey?

A dispassionate review of the facts establishes the credibility of the Hildebrand interview in terms of the individuals and organisations involved, the tenor and content of the interview and the timescales. As such it is further confirmation of Mustafa Kemal's acknowledgement of the crimes committed in the Ottoman era. This conclusion will likely dismay those who do not wish to have their founding father corroborate and acknowledge any Ottoman culpability in a horrific crime. Similarly, others who seek to tarnish the name of Mustafa Kemal and all Turks will not welcome any evidence that suggests he denigrated and abhorred the Ottoman actions.

The possibility that Halide Edib had considered participation in an assassination plot requires a re-evaluation of Mustafa Kemal's crackdown on opposition elements. The generally favoured narrative that Mustafa Kemal exploited the plot to remove all legitimate opposition is possibly too harsh. It seems likely that leading members of the PRP might have been more complicit in the attempt to remove him than previously appreciated. In the event, Mustafa Kemal succeeded killing two birds with one stone. Many former Unionists associated with the massacres were indeed hanged, whilst the PRP leadership were pardoned and exiled. Just how complicit the PRP leaders were in the plot is an area that would benefit from further evaluation. As Ataöv himself says:

> Scholarship is like a building in perpetual repair. Perpetuating the existing set of beliefs is not necessarily a scientific approach.[1]

1   Ataöv, pp. 122-23.

Bibliography

(US), Library of Congress. "Catalog of Copyright Entries. Part 1. Group 2." 32, no. Nos 1-12 (1935).

Abadan-Unat, Emine Nermin, and Deniz Kandiyoti. *Women in Turkish Society*, Vol. 30: Brill, 1981.

Adıvar, Halide Edib. *House with Wisteria: Memoirs of Halidé Edib*, Leopolis Press, 2003.

———. *The Turkish Ordeal: Being the Further Memoirs of Halidé Edib*, New York, London: The Century Company, 1928.

Akçam, Taner. *A Shameful Act: The Armenian Genocide and the Question of Turkish Responsibility*, Macmillan, 2006.

Announcement, Death. "Joseph Brainin, Journalist and Associated with Weizmann Institute, Dies at 74," *Jewish Telegraphic Agency*, 9th February 1970.

Arslan, Mark B. "Armenian Immigration Project." Shiplists, http://arslanmb.org/ArmenianImmigrants/shiplists.html - Findings.

Ataöv, Türkkaya. *The "Armenian Question": Conflict, Trauma & Objectivity*. Center for Strategic Research, 1999.

Ataöv, Türkkaya. *Armenian Falsifications*, New York: Okey Enterprises Inc, 2008.

Azak, Umut. *Islam and Secularism in Turkey: Kemalism, Religion and the Nation State*, IB Tauris, 2010.

Banki, Judith Herschcopf, and John Pawlikowski. *Ethics in the Shadow of the Holocaust: Christian and Jewish Perspectives*. Rowman & Littlefield, 2001.

Blanchard, Margaret A. *Revolutionary Sparks: Freedom of Expression in Modern America*, Oxford University Press, 1992.

Bosworth, Clifford Edmund. *The Encyclopaedia of Islam, New Edition: Supplement*. Brill Archive, 1980.

Brainin, Joseph. "Letter from Seven Arts Feature Syndicate to Herbert J. Seligmann," in *W. E. B. Du Bois Papers* edited by Seven Arts Feature Syndicate/ Worldwide News Service, 1. New York: Special Collections and University Archives, University of Massachusetts Amherst Libraries, 1931.

Burke III, Edmund. *Subversives and Mavericks in the Muslim Mediterranean: A Subaltern History*, University of Texas Press, 2016.

California, Online Archive of. "Hearst Corporation Los Angeles Examiner Photographs, Negatives and Clippings--Portrait Files (N-Z) 7000.1c, Background." California: University of Southern California.

Çalışlar, İpek. *Madam Atatürk: The First Lady of Modern Turkey*, London: Saki Books, 2013.

Carmichael, Cathie. "Was Religion Important in the Destruction of Ancient Communities in the Balkans, Anatolia and Black Sea Regions, C. 1870–1923?" *Southeast European and Black Sea Studies* 7, no. 3 (2007): 357-71.

Center, American Jewish Periodical. "Worldwide News Service & Seven Arts Feature Syndicate News," in *AJPC*. New York: Hebrew Union College/Jewish Institute of Religion, 2017.

Correspondent. "Politics Institute Calls a Feminist," *The New York Times*, 28th May 1928.

Court, US Supreme. "International News Service V. Associated Press, 248 U.S. 215 (1918)," in *No 231*, edited by US Supreme Court. Washington DC, 1918.

Cuthbert, Marlene. "Reaction to International News Agencies: 1930s and 1970s Compared," *Gazette (Leiden, Netherlands)* 26, no. 2 (1980): 99-110.

Dadrian, Vahakn N. *Documentation of the Armenian Genocide in Turkish Sources*, Institute on the Holocaust and Genocide, 1991.

Dagblad, Stockholms. "*Stockholms Dagblad Hq*," Stocholms Stad, 1913.

de Haan, Francisca, Krasimira Daskalova, and Anna Loutfi. *Biographical Dictionary of Women's Movements and Feminisms in*

Central, Eastern, and South Eastern Europe: 19th and 20th Centuries, Central European University Press, 2006.

Deringil, Selim. "Political Opposition in the Early Turkish Republic: The Progressive Republican Party 1924-1925," JSTOR, 1994.

Diggins, John Patrick. *Mussolini and Fascism: The View from America*, Princeton University Press, 2015.

Edib, Halide. *Conflict of East and West in Turkey*, (1935).

———. *The Turkish Ordeal. Being the Further Memoirs of Halide Edib*. Century Company, 1928.

Eisenstadt, Peter R. *The Encyclopedia of New York State*, Syracuse University Press, 2005.

Emil, Hildebrand Karl. *Det Gamla Och Det Nya Kina (the Old and the New China)*, Stockholm: Hugo Gebers Förlag, 1927.

Erickson, Edward J. *Mustafa Kemal Atatürk*. Bloomsbury Publishing, 2013.

Erkan, Ayça Ülker. "The Formation of Feminist Identity: Feminism in the 1930's Turkey and Britain," September, 2011.

Findley, Carter V. *Turkey, Islam, Nationalism, and Modernity: A History, 1789-2007*, Yale University Press, 2010.

Fraenkel, Max. "Adolf Hitler Explains, an Exclusive Interview with Germany's Fascist Chieftain," *The Jewish Criterion*, 23rd January 1931.

———. "Hitler Angry at Interview on Jews." *The Jewish Criterion*, 6th February 1931.

Gaiser Casey, Carrie. "The Ballet Corporealities of Anna Pavlova and Albertina Rasch," *Dance Chronicle, 35*, no. 1 (2012): 8-29.

Gawrych, George. *The Young Atatürk: From Ottoman Soldier to Statesman of Turkey*, IB Tauris, 2013.

Georgia, University System of. "The Southern Israelite Archive," in *GALILEO Scholar*. Georgia: Board of Regents of the University System of Georgia, 2017.

Global, Publishers. "United States: List of American Publishers," in *Publishers Global*, USA: PublishersGlobal, 2017.

Gocek, Fatma Muge. *Denial of Violence: Ottoman Past, Turkish Present*, *and Collective Violence against the Armenians, 1789-2009*, Oxford University Press, 2014.

Goldner, Loren. "'Socialism in One Country' before Stalin, and the Origins of Reactionary 'Anti-Imperialism': The Case of Turkey, 1917–1925." *Critique* 38, no. 4 (19th November 2010): 631-61.

Graf, Arndt, and Chua Beng Huat. *Port Cities in Asia and Europe*, Routledge, 2008.

Günergun, Feza. "Adnan Adıvar's Works in History of Science: Prior to the 'La Science Chez Les Turcs Ottomans' and Thereafter," *Osmanlı Bilimi Araştırmaları* (Studies in Ottoman Science) 7, no. 2 - 1 (2006).

Gustafsson, Karl Erik, and Per Rydén. *A History of the Press in Sweden*, Nordicom, 2010.

Halberstam, David. *Breaking News: How the Associated Press Has Covered War, Peace, and Everything Else*, Princeton Architectural Press, 2007.

Hale, William. *Turkish Politics and the Military*, Routledge, 2013.

Henderson Hay, Sara. "Seasons of the Heart," in *Quest of Faith: Poems by Sara Henderson Hay*, Princeton Theological Monograph Series, edited by Dikran Y. Hadidian, Eugene, Oregon: Pickwick Publications, 1989.

Hildebrand, Karl Emil. "Contributors Listing," in *The Encyclopedia Britannica* edited by Panel Editors, London: Encyclopedia Britannica 1922.

———. *San Antonio Light*. "'I'll Hang Every Plotter Against Turkey's Peace!' Warns Kemal," 15 August 1926.

Hildebrand, Karl Emil Hildebrand. *Johan Iii Och Europas Katolska Makter, 1568-1580: Studier I 1500-Talets Politiska Historia*, Stockholm: Almqvist & Wiksells boktryckeriaktiebolag, 1898.

Hofberg, Herman. *Svenskt Biografiskt Handlexikon* (Swedish Biographical Handbook), Stockholm: Albert Bonniers Forlag, 1909, Digitalised by Project Runeberg.

Holdwater. "Ataturk's 1926 "Interview" Proven as Forgery." http://www.tallarmeniantale.com/forger-Emile1926.htm.

Ivan, Hakim. "Is Palestine in Danger?" *The Canadian Jewish Chronicle*, 27th November 1925, p. 9.

Kim, Soo. "Chinese Confuse Sweden with Switzerland: Sweden and Switzerland Have Launched a Joint Awareness Campaign to Help Chinese Tourists Tell the Two Countries Apart," *Daily Telegraph*, 12th November 2013.

Kinross, Patrick. *Ataturk*, London: Hachette UK, 2012.

Klein, Abraham Moses. *Am Klein: The Letters*, University of Toronto Press, 2011.

Knaus, Katharina. "Turkish Women: A Century of Change," *Turkish Policy Quarterly* 6, no. 5 (2007): 47-59.

Kovarik, Bill. *Revolutions in Communication: Media History from Gutenberg to the Digital Age*, Bloomsbury Publishing USA, 2015.

Kurzman, Charles. *Modernist Islam, 1840-1940: A Sourcebook*, Oxford University Press, USA, 2002.

Macfie, Alexander Lyon. *Ataturk*, Routledge, 2014.

Malcom, Malcolm Vartan. *The Armenians in America*, Pilgrim Press, 1910.

Mango, Andrew. *Atatürk: The Biography of the Founder of Modern Turkey*, 2011.

Martel, Gordon. *The Month That Changed the World: July 1914*, Oxford: Oxford University Press (UK), 2014.

Minister, Office of the Prime. "Health Personnel Serving in the First Term of the Turkish National Assembly," Ataturk Cultural Center, http://www.atam.gov.tr/dergi/sayi-42/turkiye-millet-meclisi-birinci-doneminde-gorev-yapan-saglik-mensuplari.

Ministry of Culture, Turkey. "Ataöv, Türkkaya." http://www.kultur.gov.tr/EN,118279/ataov-turkkaya.html.

Morgenthau, Henry, *Ambassador Morgenthau's Story*, London: Gomidas Institute, 2016.

Müller-Sommerfeld, H. "The League of Nations, a-Mandates and Minority Rights During the Mandate Period in Iraq," *PDF hosted at the Radboud Repository of the Radboud University Nijmegen* (2016): 258.

News.com.au. "New Year's Eve Sex Assaults Also Reported in Finland, Sweden and Austria," News Corp Australian Network, 2016.

Obituary. "Bernard Postal Dead at 75," *Jewish Telegraphic Agency*, 9th March 1981.

————. "Joseph Brainin Is Dead at 74; Aide of Weizmann Institute." *New York Times*, 1970.

Özoğlu, Hakan. *From Caliphate to Secular State: Power Struggle in the Early Turkish Republic*, ABC-CLIO, 2011.

Paneth, Donald. *The Encyclopedia of American Journalism*, Fact of File Publications, 1983.

Piotrowski, Bernard. "Sweden and the Question of Poland's Independence (1914–1918)," (1992).

Rappaport, Helen. *Encyclopedia of Women Social Reformers*. Vol. 1: ABC-CLIO, 2001.

Reporter, Staff. "Turkish Horror." *Sunday Times (Perth)*, 18th July 1926.

Rikarkivet. "Karl E H Hildebrand." Riksarkivet, the National Archives of Sweden, https://sok.riksarkivet.se/Sbl/Presentation.aspx?id=13587 - Meriter.

Rogers, Sam L "Religious Bodies 1916, Part 2. Seperate Denominations: History, Description & Statistics," pp. 36-41. Washington: US Dept of Commerce, Bureau of the Census, 1916.

Schoolfield, George C. "Utopien Von Freiheit: Die Schweiz Im Spiegel Der Schwedischen Literatur. Beiträge Zur Nordischen Philologie 23," *Scandinavian Studies* 69, no. No 2 (Spring 1997 1997): 259-62.

Schwarzlose, Richard Allen. *The Nation's Newsbrokers: The Formative Years, from Pretelegraph to 1865*. Vol. 1: Northwestern University Press, 1989.

Sevgi Zübeyde, Gürbüz. "Some More Ugly Lies About Ataturk," *Turkish Journal* Online Edition 11/08/07 (2007).

Shaw, Stanford J. *Reform, Revolution, and Republic: The Rise of Modern*

Turkey 1808-1975, Cambridge: Cambridge University Press, 1977.

Shaw, Stanford J, and Ezel Kural Shaw. *History of the Ottoman Empire and Modern Turkey: Volume 2, Reform, Revolution, and Republic: The Rise of Modern Turkey 1808-1975*, Vol. 11: Cambridge University Press, 1977.

Shefter, Martin. *Capital of the American Century: The National and International Influence of New York City*, Russell Sage Foundation, 1993.

Shissler, A Holly. *Between Two Empires: Ahmet Agaoglu and the New Turkey*, IB Tauris, 2002.

Silver, Jonathan D. "Hollywood's Dominance of the Movie Industry: How Did It Arise and How Has It Been Maintained?", Queensland University of Technology 2007.

Sitton, Tom. *Metropolis in the Making: Los Angeles in the 1920s*, University of California Press, 2001.

Sonyel, Salahi R. "Mustafa Kemal and Enver in Conflict, 1919–22," *Middle Eastern Studies* 25 no. 4 (1989): 506-15.

Spender, John Alfred. *The Changing East*, Cassell and Company, Ltd., 1926.

Spender, John, Alfred. *Österns Förvand ling*, Stockholm: Geber, 1927.

Sterling, Christopher H. *Encyclopedia of Journalism*, 6 vols., Vol. 1, Thousand Oaks, California: SAGE Publications Inc, 2009.

Susskind, Ron. "Faith, Certainty and the Presidency of George W. Bush," *New York Times Magazine*, 17th October 2004.

Syndicate, Chicago Tribune Co. Copyright. "Turkish Women Nominated," *New York Times*, 2nd March 1925.

Syndicate, Worldwide News. "Liquidation of Birobidjan Plans Denied by Soviet: Interview by Seven Arts Editor Burings Light on Questionable Status," *The Southern Israelite*, 1937.

Ulgen, Fatma. "Reading Mustafa Kemal Atatürk on the Armenian Genocide of 1915," *Patterns of Prejudice* 44, no. 4 (2010): 369-91.

University, Linköping. "Af Wirsén, Carl Einar Thure," *Project Runeberg* V W - Viroulet-Fagerström (2017).

Vahide, Sukran. *Islam in Modern Turkey: An Intellectual Biography of Bediuzzaman Said Nursi*, SUNY Press, 2012.

Volkan, Vamik. *Blind Trust: Large Groups and Their Leaders in Times of Crisis and Terror*, Pitchstone Publishing (US & CA), 2014.

Wachs, Martin. "Autos, Transit, and the Sprawl of Los Angeles: The 1920s," *Journal of the American Planning Association* 50, no. 3 (1984): 297-310.

Wagner, Rob Leicester. *Red Ink, White Lies: The Rise and Fall of Los Angeles Newspapers, 1920-1962*, Dragonflyer Press, 2000.

Yilmaz, Şuhnaz. "An Ottoman Warrior Abroad: Enver Paşa as an Expatriate," *Middle Eastern Studies* 35, no. 4 (1999): 40-69.

Zürcher, Erik J. *Turkey: A Modern History*, IB Tauris, 2004.

———. *The Young Turk Legacy and Nation Building: From the Ottoman Empire to Atatürk's Turkey*, Vol. 87: IB Tauris, 2014.

Zürcher, Erik J, and Touraj Atabaki. "Men of Order: Authoritarian Modernization under Ataturk and Reza Shah," London: IB Tauris & Co, 2004.

Zürcher, Erik Jan. "Atatürk as a Young Turk," *New Perspectives on Turkey*, 41 (2009): 211-26.

———. *Political Opposition in the Early Turkish Republic: The Progressive Republican Party, 1924-1925*, Vol. 44, Leiden; New York: EJ Brill, 1991.

———. *A Question of Genocide: Armenians and Turks at the End of the Ottoman Empire*, edited by Ronald Grigor Suny, Fatma Müge Göçek and Norman M Naimark. Oxford: Oxford University Press, 2011.

———. *The Unionist Factor: The Role of the Committee of Union and Progress in the Turkish National Movement, 1905-1926*, Leiden: E. J. Brill, 1984.

ABOUT THE AUTHOR:

Philip M. Pedley is a British PhD researcher and lecturer in the Politics, Philosophy and Religion Department at the University of Lancaster in the UK. He holds a degree in Politics and an MA in Diplomacy and International Relations. He has presented and published papers on the Anglosphere and the Anglo-US Special Relationship which represent his main areas of interest. In addition to his academic studies, he has had a thirty year career in business, working for a range of businesses, as well as an active life in politics. In the 1980's he was elected National Chairman of the Conservative Party's youth wing and stood as a candidate in the 1983 General Election.

Gomidas Institute
42 Blythe Rd.
London W14 0HA
United Kingdom
www.gomidas.org
info@gomidas.org

www.ingramcontent.com/pod-product-compliance
Lightning Source LLC
Chambersburg PA
CBHW031931080426
42734CB00007B/627